What We Bury At Night

What We Bury At Night

DISPOSABLE HUMANITY

Julian Aguon

blue ocean press

tokyo

Published by:

blue ocean press, an Imprint of Aoishima Research Institute (ARI)
#807-36 Lions Plaza Ebisu
3-25-3 Higashi, Shibuya-ku
Tokyo, Japan 150-0011

mail@aoishima-research.com
URL: http://www.aoishima-research.com

ISBN: 978-4-902837-67-6

TABLE OF CONTENTS

*Sometimes I believe beauty
is the only thing that keeps
me alive*
Cec Sheoships

INTRODUCTION

As the War Without End rages on, as the death toll climbs and coffins carrying dead dreams come more than the rain, as all words of diplomacy are robbed of worth, as militarization enters a new phase of manic, America's greatest export—a culture of Nothing built on reckless individualism, consumerism, and amnesia—is eating the folk of the world. Chewing us up and spitting us out, different. Hollowed.

While the world looks away, an entire region of the planet is facing down death. Mostly losing. Passing in the night.

Micronesia, home to civilizations born up to 2,000 years before Jesus, is being disappeared. Wiped clean from the Western Pacific. Made up of more than 2,000 islands and atolls in three major archipelagos—the Carolines, the Marshalls, and the Marianas—Micronesia was known from the last World War until the 1970s as the Trust Territory of the Pacific Islands. All of it—the Republic of the Marshall Islands (RMI), the Federated States of Micronesia (FSM), the Republic of Palau (Belau), and the Commonwealth of the Northern Mariana Islands (CNMI)—less Guam, which was cut from the rest after the Spanish-American war and lumped

9

with the other 1898 Unfortunates: the Philippines, Puerto Rico, and Cuba.

Historically, our strategic location so close to the Asian continent, our value as the U.S.' westernmost possession has meant our involuntary participation in all the wars of recent history: World War II, Vietnam, Korea, the Gulf, Afghanistan, the Horn of Africa, Iraq. In this current chapter, All Eyes on China, our role remains: The Geo Political Gems. Empire's Darlings.

Of late the name is Lily Pad. Home—landing base, service station, testing grounds, launch pad—to the War Frog.

In 2007, we who sailed the Pacific for four millennia, mostly surviving the machinations of the old school colonizers, today look like Hagar—desperate to find water in a desert. Lining up at a table of foodlessness expecting, hoping, dying, to be fed. Our trust turned against us. If the nuclear testing program wherein the U.S. dropped 67 atomic bombs on the Marshall Islands and then used our Marshallese kin as human radiation experiments was not enough an indicia that we have a less than friendly friend in the U.S., the Solomon Report of 1963—wherein the permanent crippling of our political economies was laid out, and adopted, as the official

U.S. policy with regard to Micronesia—should have closed the case.

But as a region we have been reared on a diet of dispossession. Of liberation day parades and cleverly put-together versions of history wherein the US is always the god, we the grateful.

Despite that the history of the U.S. presence in our islands is an increasingly documented, increasingly disturbing one, many Micronesians continue to cling to the illusion of alliance. Desperate to behold in it the face of the Friend.

But the stakes are higher than before, indeed, then they have ever been. The new wave of US-led militarization of the Pacific has dealt a cruel hand and the chips are our children. And to them we have passed a tragic torch: to date, Micronesians serve—and die—in the U.S. military at the highest rate in the entire U.S. In societies once celebrated for the richness of our stories and story-telling, a narrative of Virulent Visionlessness has gripped us. And the young are the ones telling it. Just this morning (July 27, 2007) the Guam Air National Guard swore in 20 more from Guam in one of the largest groups enlisted at one time in the past several years. [1] Though this fiscal year's authorized enlistment is 281, the Guard is now at 372 members and

11

counting. [2] The Guard has far exceeded its authorized enlistment figure every year for the last half decade. [3] Last year, the Guard raked in 337. [4] 319 the year before that. [5] And that's just the Guard. When it comes to Guam, recruiters from the Army, Air Force, Coast Guard, and Navy all have bragging rights. Amid crashing economies, deplorable minimum wages, salaries that haven't been raised since the 70s, failed and floundering attempts at development based on Asian Development Bank and other western theories of development that do not work in subsistence-based, non-cash economies, a chilling sound can be heard. The sound of children crying at the funerals of their imaginations.

As the international community still fails to apprehend—an oversight no doubt enjoying its last days—Micronesia may literally mean 'the tiny islands' but nothing is small about our vital importance to the accelerating needs of the U.S. war project, and by consequence, our potential to seriously interrupt it.

In Kwajalein, where the U.S. homeports its Intercontinental Ballistic Missile (ICBM) technology, the fight is on. All signs point to a refusal on the part of the Kwajalein landowners to renew the agreement by which the U.S. may lease the atoll until 2086. In Guam—where the U.S. is set to have its second round of enormous-scale Valiant Shield military exercises as well as its full-scale anti-terrorism TOPOFF 4 exercises—even some senators are outraged that the U.S. initially suggested that Guam, its Colony in Perpetuity, would foot the $10 million bill to host the war games when we cannot even confidently pledge to pay our teachers on time.[6]

That Micronesia is one of the last corners on earth where people, on the whole, still pattern life in humane and interdependent arrangements built on sustaining, life-supporting values (in short, where people still mostly function as people) says something—perhaps that there is something about us that is wildly resilient.[7] Perhaps it is an offering of beauty that is our contribution to the world. A gift for the whole, from the part.

This book follows Micronesia as I, a son of her, traveled her. It begins in the Marshall Islands, where the history of the nuclear testing program is the boldest of U.S. brutality in the region and where today indignation burns bright. It then moves to the FSM where crushing poverty has meant much in the way of malnutrition—of body and imagination. Then to Belau, where an activist history of courage in the face of enormous odds both nourishes and takes veils from those tempted to misread the politics of power. Then to the Chamorus of the CNMI and Guam, who are set to weather a

13

storm of massive U.S. military buildup, which marks a turning point in the war on terror and means to be decisive. Then, a word about magic. That thing for which our young are so hungry. It is to them whom I dedicate this work.

Finally, use of the word "we" in this book cannot be helped. I am connected to these people, whose stories of struggle, of mourning, of losing, of winning relief in small but shining moments, are also my own.

We will survive, or go out, together.

*fictitious names have been used in this report to protect the confidentiality of persons.

Note to Reader: After World War II, the United Nations conferred upon the United States the sacred obligation of guiding the islands comprising the former Trust Territory of the Pacific Islands (the Marshall Islands, the Federated States of Micronesia, Palau (Belau), and the Northern Mariana Islands) toward self-governance. In 1947, the U.S. took on the international responsibility to terminate the colonial status of these islands in accordance with the highest norm of international law: self-determination. It accepted the same charge the year before with regard to Guam, its colony since 1898. The following addresses how the Trustee has fared.

Of Mice, Not Men

On the Marshall Islands

*The Republic of the Marshall Islands (RMI) gained
independence in 1986 with the signing of its Compact of Free
Association (Compact I) with the United States. Under
Compact I, the U.S. retained its mili-political stronghold of
the RMI through strategic denial, a policy designed to allow
U.S. military access to Micronesian states formerly entrusted
to them while denying any other Power such access. In
exchange for an ability to "volunteer" for service in the U.S.
armed forces, visa-free travel in and out of the U.S., access
to certain federal programs and other U.S. economic aid, the
U.S. manages the RMI's foreign affairs and provides them
military defense. Since the end of WWII, the U.S. military has
housed the Ronald Reagan Ballistic Missile Defense Test
Site, its test facility for missile defense and space research
programs, in Kwajalein atoll. After Compact I ended in
2001, the RMI government underwent negotiations resulting
in the passage of the second Compact of Free Association
(Compact II) in 2003, which is far less favorable to the RMI.
With the Cold War over and the U.S. as the unchallenged
superpower of the world, RMI negotiators had less political
leverage to hold the U.S. to its obligations under Compact I.
Compact II releases the U.S. from the obligation to provide*

compensation for survivors of its Nuclear Testing Program,
which detonated 67 nuclear bombs in the Marshalls. Though
the U.S. hawked that nuclear testing needed to be done in the
Marshalls for the good of all mankind, the Marshallese
people are left with the bill—continuing to die of
radioactivity-related cancers at horrific rates. The fund set
up to cover the anticipated subsequent medical care is nearly
extinguished and the Bush administration maintains that the
U.S. owes them nothing.

Immediately after the last world war, when the U.S. was first entrusted with the fate of the people of Micronesia, it began an intense nuclear bombing campaign on the Marshall Islands, dropping 67 nuclear bombs. If you take the output of the radioactive energy yield of these 67 bombs, it is the rough equivalent of 1.7 Hiroshima shots every day for 12 years.[8] Most of the bombs dropped on the Marshall Islands during the Nuclear Testing Program (NTP) from 1946-1958 lifted radioactive sediment into the sky and powdered it on surrounding areas, putting it in clouds where it traveled thousands of miles and rained on people.[9]

I was fishing for mackerel in the morning with my grandfather when the bomb was dropped. I was nine, but something like that you never forget. I was carrying the basket for my grandfather. I don't know how to describe it, but we knew immediately that something was wrong. We knew that tests were being done, bombs were being dropped. We had seen and heard some of them before. But this was different. Everything seemed to happen within a few seconds. In my mind it all happened within the space of a few seconds. It was not a boom. Atomic and hydrogen bombs don't do that. They don't boom. They rumble. Like thunder. The sky turned completely red. And this was about 6 o'clock in the morning. It was like

19

someone had put me and my grandfather in a glass bowl and poured blood in it. The beach was red, the ocean was red, the fish in my basket was red. I peed in my pants. I grabbed my grandfather and he threw everything down and half-carried me back to the house. My aunty normally ran our household but she was not on Likiep at the time; she was on Majuro. My grandfather gave me and my cousin two pieces of rebar to go bang on the community bell, which was an oxygen tank hanging from a tree, calling everyone to the house. We were so confused. It was supposed to be daylight but it was deep red like blood. I think what may have been a blessing for us is that my grandfather had an old radio we all gathered around. School was let out. There was no activity. My grandfather pulled down all the water catchment containers and we didn't drink the water for the next few days though it was raining. The water falling on Likiep was too radioactive. There was a small school on Likiep with kids from all over the Marshalls there. And to the north, in Utirik, and Utirik is farther away from ground zero than we were, they evacuated the people. I believe, actually all the documents indicate, that Ailuk was exposed as much as Utirik was, but the U.S. did not evacuate them because there were too many of them. They had enough guinea pigs.

...62-year-old Marshallese man speaking about being a child in Likiep, roughly 165 miles from Ground

20

Zero, when the U.S. dropped Bravo—the worst of the 67 nuclear bombs detonated in the Marshalls.

Many Marshallese people who never went to college could quote without blinking former National Security Advisor and Secretary of State Henry Kissinger's summary of the U.S. attitude toward these islands:

> There are only 90,000 people out there. Who gives a damn?[10]
> ...H.K. on the bombing of the Marshalls.

More chilling are the words of one of the leading Atomic Energy Commission (AEC) scientists, regarding the use of Marshallese people as human radiation experiments:

> [I]t will be very interesting to go back and get good environmental data, how many per square mile; what isotopes are involved and a sample of food changes in many humans through their urines, so as to get a measure of the human uptake when people live in a contaminated environment. Now, data of this type has never been available. While it is true that these people do not live, I would say, the way Westerners do, civilized people, it is nevertheless also true that these people are more like us than the mice. So that is something which will be done this winter.[11]

21

...Dr. Merrill Eisenbud.

Years later this doctor, sitting in on one of the subsequent hearings between the U.S. and the RMI governments, would quietly sob as this information was presented to the committee.[12]

Some are too tired to cry.

> You know, I used to cry when I talk about it but not anymore. I'm tired. I have problems still. I try to take care of myself. I'm taking the Synthroid medicine everyday of my life for the thyroid. All my thyroids have been taken out. They have moved five glands. I think I have another one growing. But if they take that out they're going to take everything away and leave me nothing to live on. But I was lucky because when they operate on people, like on other women, it gave them a soft voice, and flat. They don't sing anymore. They soft. Pretty soon they will never have any voice. I used to be a singer. I used to have a group who sang in Kwajalein. We sang in church and for fundraising and for the FM radio. There used to be a band called Jeremy and friends. He was my boyfriend. I was 27. He was a little younger than me. I was living on Ebeye.

I am very tired. My whole story and my whole song I have been singing everyday of my life and I'm sick and tired of it. I am very, very sick and tired of hearing myself singing the same song, same story. Many people from the U.S., Japan, Europe, from anywhere, they keep coming back and asking me the same questions and I say: 'what happened to the people who interviewed with me? What did they do with my story before? How come they didn't let the world know? They didn't share it?' It's crazy.

...61-year-old Rongelapese woman.

Remembering Bravo, she says:

They knew the wind was going to change. The weathermen said it. They evacuated us later. They waited another one day and a half before they came. They bring goats and animals on the ships. They didn't act so quickly because they wanted us to drink the water when it changed color. They wanted to use us as a guinea pig. They needed someone to study. That's why they didn't act so quickly. They were waiting for us to eat the powder and drink the water so the radiation goes in our stomachs and our bodies so they can study us.

The old myth was that the wind shifted direction. But efforts in the early 80s to declassify information through the

23

Freedom of Information Act proved that American weathermen on Rongerik atoll gave a midnight weather report on the morning of Bravo, reporting that winds were blowing straight toward them. Because the test was not done until after 6 a.m. the next morning, it is beyond doubt that this was no accident. As one writer at the *Marshall Islands Journal* puts it:

> It was March 1 or bust. This helps us understand that it wasn't just the Marshallese. There was also a group of American weathermen on Rongerik and they got doused too. They weren't evacuated. What this tells me is that health was just not an issue then. With exposed groups, the U.S. now had control groups to study. The Cold War mentality coupled with the fact that Russia blew one up a year before the U.S. was enough for the latter to proceed with the drop, irrespective of peoples' health, Marshallese or American.

As far as the U.S. government was concerned, it was dropping bombs on mice, not men.

A 1953 document lists U.S. government studies to be associated with a new series of atomic and hydrogen tests; Project 4.1 was the designation of the medical study of Marshallese people exposed to the radioactive fallout of

24

Bravo. That year, it was titled "Study of Response of Human Beings Exposed to Significant Beta and Gamma Radiation Due to Fall-Out from High Yield Weapons."[13] The next year, a few days after Bravo, the same was re-titled "Study of Response of Human Beings *Accidentally* Exposed to Significant Fallout Radiation."[14] [emphasis added]. As one former Marshallese Minister of Foreign Affairs recalls:

> For years and years they denied ever carrying out Project 4.1, except we had pictures of people of Rongelap holding up placards on their chest that say Project 4.1.

> Brookhaven National Laboratory in New York. They told the people they were being taken to a hospital but that's not a hospital. That's a laboratory. We have pictures of them being herded like animals.

Of course the trick was too cheap. People don't just forget the day their world dies. Parents tell children. Grandmothers hold stories until small boys can hear them:

> A lot of my aunties and uncles and both my grandparents were there at the time and suffered from the fallout. Hair falling off, skin peeling off. They were the closest group of people within vicinity of ground zero and the sad thing about it is that the U.S.

25

government exploded previous tests in 1946 and 1948, which were less strong than the 1954 shot, yet they evacuated us to other atolls. But for Bravo, we were put back on Rongelap and despite knowing that the wind was shifting toward us and that the Bravo shot was much stronger than previous tests, they went ahead and exploded it without moving us. We had all kinds of radiogenic conditions. Beta burns, nausea.

One of the first victims, the Anjain boy, died in a hospital in the U.S. He suffered leukemia and that's when people started to confirm their theories that they were being used as subjects, like guinea pigs to be studied on. Later we found out that some of us who were not part of the exposed population—people from Rongelap but who were not there at the time of the Bravo shot—were injected with chromium. These people were used as a comparison group with the exposed group. We have documents wherein the U.S. has admitted to injecting some of our people with chromium 51 and tritium liquid which we were forced to drink. It was like taking a person to the hospital and x-raying them even if they didn't have a medical condition. The amount of radiation we received from Bravo was equivalent to placing a person in an x-ray room and shooting them with 25,000 shots with no protection...The first victim died a couple of years later. The majority of our people have thyroid operations, cancers, continue to suffer. It is very significant that the population is small but the rate of radiogenic diseases is very high. There's no question about this.

...Mayor of Rongelap, speaking about the nuclear testing program.

Another Rongelapese man, 54, says that in all his adult life he knows of only two individuals—himself and another man—who have not had a thyroid removed. He shares:

I was two years old. As I grew up, when I started maturing, my grandmother told me everything. I was only a child and I didn't know I went through all that. I learned more about it. I went to school, heard it from different people old enough at that time. She told me I was very sick after the Bravo shot. Diarrhea, vomiting, my hair was coming out, my skin was coming off, and I was very, very sick. They had no medicine. After the shot, when we moved to Kwajalein, all they would treat us with is making us swim in the beach and wash us because we were so itchy. When you scratched, your skin comes off. When you have itchy hair, your hair comes out. Everyone from Rongelap moved to Kwajalein first, then Majuro. Then they moved us back in 1957. A couple of other people who were not exposed also moved back to Rongelap with us. My mother was

27

one of them. Then everyone moved off of Rongelap to Majeto in 1985 with the assistance of Greenpeace because it was too contaminated. Every year we'd receive medical attention from the Department of Energy (DOE). Used to be called Atomic Energy Commission (AEC). You know what they told me? I would not live long. Well, I'm still here and I'm very thankful for it.

The same man goes on to expose an unrecorded history of how Project 4.1 did not die when it should have:

When I was in college in New Mexico, one time this DOE doctor came. I don't know how he found out that I was in New Mexico, but he came out and took me to New York to Brookhaven National Laboratory and I stayed with a lot of sick people. I lived with them for two weeks. They were retarded people. They were mentally and physically sick. Some were very nervous, and crazy and all that. They were sick. They examined me and examined my throat and put me into some kind of radiation tests. And the people were telling me: 'Why? Why are you here? You are very healthy. You don't look sick.' They were wondering why I was there in the compound. Some of them couldn't speak so they write down, asking questions, saying: 'why are you here? You look healthy. Why are you here with us?' Sometimes some

of them asked me to help them turn on the t.v. They
were sick. I stayed with them two weeks then I went
back to New Mexico.

They drew blood, did x-rays. And in the end, they
didn't tell me much. They told me they'd be back to
conduct further examinations. But they didn't come
back.

Did they ever call you? No.
Did you ever see any piece a paper? No.
You know nothing about the results? No.

One Rongelapese woman, 61, who keeps an old photograph
of her grandmother in her purse, hits the nail on the head of
the U.S.-Marshallese relationship:

My grandmother was 117 years old when she died.
She was holding her Department of Energy ID
number. Everybody had a number. So when you die
of cancer, they don't write the name, just the number.
When they do their reports on the people, they don't
write our names, they only write our numbers.

In many ways, Project 4.1 continues today. The DOE
continues to pay for a special medical program for exposed
people. The same woman shares:

Till now, they use us as guinea pigs. Like Straub Hospital in Hawaii. They fly us there just for the thyroid. Other cancers, no. They get us to physically exam but not treat us, just physically exam. They knew that inside there was a problem but still they had to let the cancer grow so they know how many years we have to live with the cancer, but they don't treat. They let it grow every year...They knew how long we had to live and then watched us die. So they get educated from learning, from using us as guinea pigs. We need something in return because the choice is ours. It is with us.

The same woman continues:

We have received cancers, thyroids, leukemia, jellyfish babies, all that stuff. Still. It still happens. The U.S. still denies their radioactive plans. There are women who still give birth to jellyfish babies now. It is going to be worse than ever. According to the scientists, in a few generations from now there will be ones that look like apes or something, especially from the radioactive islands like Rongelap. According to the scientists, the radioactive poisons are going to get worse. Like in Japan, those people who were affected by radioactive poison are not allowed to marry outsiders. They marry together because their generation is going to be like that. They

made that law there. These days, the young kids feel
fine. But it started in 1980-something. They stopped
them from getting married.

They have to give us something in return for our
children. Not for us. It's too late for me. They can use
me. They can take me as I am. Take my body to use
it anywhere, but not my children. The future. That's
what I need. To know they won't be used as guinea
pigs. They could take my body and tear it apart and
share it with all the world to study with, but not my
children. I need something for my children's future
health.

But the prayer has fallen on hard hearts. The Bush
Administration has made its position clear—the $150 million
settlement reached between the U.S. and RMI governments
during Compact of Free Association negotiations was a final
settlement. [15] In fairness, the agreement was in part based on
an assumption that the Fund would be invested with the
performance goal of producing for each year of the Fund
annual average proceeds of at least $18 million dollars, to be
distributed in whole or partial payment of monetary awards
made by the Nuclear Claims Tribunal. In that way, the U.S.
could argue that the settlement amount was really $18
million dollars a year in perpetuity. But that's not the way the
cookie crumbled. Furthermore, the stickier part of the

agreement was that all Marshallese claims against the U.S. for nuclear compensation were to be extinguished. Of course, key information was kept from the RMI negotiators at the time of settlement. The settlement, known as the 177 agreement, was based on the 1978 "Northern Marshalls Radiological Study," which the U.S. claimed during negotiations to be the most complete and comprehensive study of radiation in the Marshalls ever completed.[16] Against evidence released from 1994 onward, the U.S. continues to argue that only four atolls (Bikini, Enewetak, Rongelap, and Utirik) were affected by the Nuclear Testing Program (NTP). The infamous 2005 Congressional hearings on the petition for just compensation for NTP survivors showcased how hard, how unchanged, the U.S. position really is. In that meeting, the State Department representative answered almost every question put to him by saying he had no authority to answer it.[17] He skirted the clearest questions with the fiercest ambiguity. For the State Department, perfect form.

It's not complicated really. Article IX of the Compact provides that the people of the Marshalls can file a petition with the U.S. government if circumstances that alter the fairness of the terms arise after settlement was reached, and additional compensation is appropriate. In 2000, they did just that. They filed a Changed Circumstances petition with the

U.S. Congress. After sitting on it for some four years, Congress sent it to the Bush administration for review, which led to two hearings in the summer of 2005, where it has since died.[18] Granted, part of the reason for the current dormancy is that one RMI representative wrongly responded to one Senator's question. When asked what he wanted next, he responded that the RMI government wanted to be able to negotiate this matter with the administration.[19] The answer was fatal. The Bush administration does not negotiate—not with terrorists, not even with Americans, definitely not with mice.

But the 177 agreement has other holes in it. As one former Compact negotiator puts it:

> Under the agreement, the U.S. expunged its obligations to pay for any additional claims arising over and above the specified amount. Anything over would be RMI responsibility. But how can a dependent territory be required to expunge claims against a mother colonial power while it is still a territory, when the damage occurred in a territory state?

> The problem is not whether it was a good deal or not but that it was a *sine quo non* of the Compact. The US basically said: 'if you don't accept this deal, and

expunge us, then there will be no Compact, no termination of trusteeship, and you will be a trust territory forever.' At that time, RMI negotiators conceded because our elders at the time desired an end to the trusteeship.

Only last month (June 2007), a group of activists pleaded with the U.S. Congress to take some measure. Public Advocate at the Majuro-based Nuclear Claims Tribunal (NCT) says:

> The petition submitted in 2000 has went nowhere. Congress has done nothing, but it could provide compensation on an *ex gratia* basis if it wanted. We'll close down. Our files hopefully will be stored in a place where it won't be eaten by termites or destroyed by the elements.

This year, the NCT is set to close its doors. Established in 1988 pursuant to the Compact to adjudicate nuclear compensation claims, the tribunal has about $900,000 left, which will carry it only to the end of the year.[20] While on one hand, a good deal of the personal injury awards has been paid out, some as much as 91%, there is still an unpaid balance of $18 million dollars.[21] This is nothing when compared to unpaid property damage claims, which include a $563 million award for Bikini and a $386 million award for

34

Enewetak.[22] That is without interest. In December 2006, $300 million was awarded to Utirik.[23] Only two months ago (May 2007), Rongelap was awarded a $1 billion dollar award.[24]

Worse, the National Cancer Institute released a study in September 2004 estimating that among the population of people living in the Marshalls at the time of the NTP, there would be an increase of 500 cancers in a population of 14,000.[25] At the time of its release, only half of these cancers had yet to manifest.

There is too much we don't know about these tests. And when we get close, we get burned.

In 1994, President Clinton set up an advisory committee to look into the history of various government-sanctioned human radiation experiments. Its work was cut short the next year, as Republicans took office and reduced funding. In its time, the committee stumbled on a key finding: the U.S. government used mental patients, kids with disabilities, Alaskan natives, black prisoners, etc., in its experiments, while giving the Atomic Energy Commission a pass for the Nuclear Testing Program in the Marshalls.[26]

This pattern no doubt colors Marshallese distrust of the U.S. government when it says, for example, that certain atolls are now inhabitable.

Rongelap is still hot. One estimate puts inhabitability at 25,000 years.[27] Yet there's a movement to resettle the Rongelapese. The U.S. Department of Justice claims that it is now safe to re-settle some of the islands.[28] But folks want President Bush and the Congress to declare that. They want assurances. After all, they have been moved back before and that didn't exactly pan out. In 1957, only three years after Bravo, they were taken back to Rongelap, where they were built a church, a school, and, in poor form, a camp for American scientists to continue to study them.[29]

> The U.S. is supposed to have ongoing monitoring programs to make sure radiation levels remain safe and that people are not exposed to any leakages or leaching of stored plutonium, americium, beryllium, and all the other heavy metals that give us reason for concern. Cesium should be over by now. The problem now in Enewetak and Rongelap is that the U.S. is not even monitoring these.
>
> The common sense way to know things aren't right is the supplemental food program whereby the U.S. acknowledges the danger of eating only local food,

that they should eat a mix between local food and imported food. I am so adamantly opposed to moving people back to Rongelap.

...62-year-old Marshallese man, on the resettlement of Rongelap.

Today, talk of resettling Rongelap and Enewetak is even more complicated, as the U.S. claims it has no responsibility to monitor the people who resettle or their living environment. And there's always the Bikini resettlement to cause pause. There, people were prematurely returned and then re-evacuated because their urine contained unexpectedly high levels of cesium and strontium.[30] There, as a safety measure, the strategy was to add gravel to their living areas so as to distance playing children from the contaminated soil beneath them.[31] But children will be children; they dug and played in the dirt and got sick.

Another fact should be remembered: half of the bombs were dropped after the people of Rongelap were moved back in '57.[32]

Meanwhile, folks have been demanding other information, as all things NTP have been and still are so closely guarded. As one Marshallese Senator remarks:

If you ask for hard copy records of initial AEC records on the Marshalls, you'll find out that at least half a dozen fires are associated with these records. Even here, three fires on Majuro just happened to blow up DOE records, hospital records, and other records of the government pertaining to the NTP.

More documents are under lock and key.

Two lawsuits now in the U.S. Federal District Court of Claims include a demand of Marshallese claimants that the U.S. government declassify documents including the Tommie McCraw and the Roger Ray collections, said to contain important data about the NTP. According to one member of the RMI Parliament, the U.S. admits there are such collections but refuses to turn them over under the guise of national security. These class actions, brought by the peoples of Bikini and Enewetak, await ruling as to whether their claims have merit. Last month (June 2007), the judge came back with a finding that more information was needed for the Marshallese charge of a Fifth Amendment taking.[33]

The U.S. is not afraid of Russia, China, or outer space. But they're scared shitless of their courts. That's really where we should have stuck to our guns. The courts may take a long time, some of us may be dead by the time they come to any kind of conclusion, but that is the best way to preserve the paper trail and to force the U.S. to cough up the evidence that we don't already have. If this was a criminal case, the other guy would hang already.

...62-year-old Marshallese man in Majuro.

So it goes that people mutilated by the instruments of the powerful must hang their hopes on a judgment that has little to do with justice. Women who have buried too many babies in the night deserve better.

> Grape babies—the scientific name is *hydatiform moles*. They occur in like one in 2 million cases and we've had like 20 of them in Likiep. Some women have repeatedly given birth to these. Marie had. There are so many people I know, even from school, that have had grape babies. So what do they do? They go bury them. In the middle of the night. Baby, mother, grandmother, and midwife. They don't want the rest of the world to know. And now the Americans come and say: 'if this was such a great problem, how come these people don't talk about it.' Well, it was US policy to keep this information down and anybody who spoke out was a communist. I was in still high school when Ana told me about the two babies who were still in their mother's womb when they were given Project 4.1 numbers.
>
> ...62-year-old Marshallese man.

39

These babies were given numbers before they were given names. Until 1973, other babies were treated like monkeys.

> When the AEC doctors were first brought out to pull out teeth of young children, we thought that they were fixing our teeth when they were really just pulling them to determine how much cesium and strontium were in the enamel of the teeth. You know how they told us to open our mouth to get our teeth: *Olongi Monkey* (open your mouth monkey). How can people not feel like apes? And they were doing this until 1973. They were still pulling healthy teeth out of Marshallese children claiming to be fixing their teeth when in fact they were just studying how radiation spreads.
>
> ...62-year-old Marshallese man.

But these days, the fight is on. The RMI government has made a promise it cannot keep: Kwajalein.

In 2004, without the necessary approval of the Kwajalein landowners, the RMI and the U.S. governments signed a new Military Use and Operating Rights Agreement (MUORA) therein giving the latter the option to renew its right to lease Kwajalein atoll until 2086.[34] Under the new MUORA, the U.S. will pay Kwajalein landowners roughly $15 million dollars.[35] The MUORA, however, cannot take effect without

40

a new Land Use Agreement (LUA) between the landowners and RMI government. And all the signs say nay. Many of these landowners have been relocated to Ebeye, where close to 15,000 people are crammed onto a tenth of a square mile.[36] One estimate sets the number of persons living in one house in the densest district of Ebeye at 45.[37] According to a 2003 Asian Development Bank publication, only one student out of 97 passed the public high school entrance exam that year. Weekly water shortages, daily power fluctuations, widespread malnutrition, kids surfing on discarded plywood are but a glimpse. As one Marshallese elder puts it:

> They're putting people in hardship positions, denying them access to what they need to keep up their indigenous habits and traditions. People on Bikini now no longer know how to sail. Pretty soon the people of Kwajalein will be the same way. They're denying them the environment where their spirit can continue to live. That is the worst thing. It's one thing to move people from one island to another, and another to move them and deny that access they need to keep up their humanity as they know it. That is the worst thing the military has done: move people from their place of birth, their traditional homes, their traditional fishing grounds, their traditional farms, and you might as well kill 'em. True they'll have money, a nice office on Majuro, a nice home on Long

Island, but that's not their home. It's a temporary place of residence until they can get home again. And how temporary is temporary when the damage is thousands of years? It's damage so permanent in terms of environment and spirit, there's no way to pay for it.

A ten minute boat ride away—where teens of Ebeye go to work menial jobs, where small boys go to fill water jugs because Ebeye is out—the contrast is sharp. According to one Marshallese Senator, there are only a dozen military personnel on Kwajalein, while the rest are scientists making an average salary of about $75,000 for the development of star wars technology.[38]

When the first Compact ended, Kwajalein landowners were receiving about $11 million a year total. The first year of Compact II was $15 million dollars, but because they have not signed a new LUA, they are not entitled to higher rent.[39] While they are still getting paid according to the old LUA, the difference between the $11 and $15 million figures, which every year is being adjusted for inflation, is being thrown into an escrow account.[40] According to one writer at the Marshall Islands Journal, this account is worth about $12 million and is now being used essentially to coerce them to sign the new LUA.

Here's the rub: if there is no agreement by 2009, congressional legislation says the money goes back to the U.S. As the same writer puts it: "the carrot is hanging out there but so is the hammer that's going to go boom, down on them in two years."[41]

Recently, in response to a June 26, 2007 interview with former U.S. Ambassador to the RMI, William Bodde, Jr., one Kwajalein Senator writes:

> As to Kwajalein, our rejection of a new Land Use Agreement is not based solely on the lease payments proposed by the U.S. Government. When we rejected a renewal of the lease beyond 2016, all offers were taken off the table, including the 19.1 million that is so often cited by reporters like those in Hawaii public radio. Kwajalein, in our view, is but one component of the overall package that is the Compact.

More importantly, he writes:

> The Kwajalein people watch, with great interest, the plight of the people of Bikini and Enewetak, Rongelap and Utirik and ask themselves, "Is this what happens to people who give their all to the United States?" By some estimates, nearly 40% of the Marshallese people are displaced by virtue of U.S. military activities in the islands. Rentals are not what

43

Kwajalein is all about. Anyone who has visited Kwajalein and seen the living conditions in the labor camp on Ebeye will agree that this situation cannot continue for another 70 years.

And it's not just Kwajalein. Compact II is One Helluva Mess. The same Senator writes:

> Compact 2 removes the more significant of American obligations to the people it subjugated to nuclear ambitions while attempting to render permanent Marshallese obligations to the United States. Compensation and medical care promised to the people who suffered the insult of the equivalent of 1.7 Hiroshimas every day for twelve years have been shoved aside in Compact 2 by heavy handed American negotiators intimidating Marshallese counterparts. Basic benefits unique to the relationship, such as postal services, [Federal Emergency Management Agency], or FEMA, scholarships and other Compact provisions designed to make up for the stunted growth the islands suffered under [the Department of Interior's] trusteeship administration have been eliminated. Our concerns about environmental degradation in Kwajalein are not being addressed.

The first clue should be that it took only two years to negotiate, whereas Compact I negotiations lasted 17 years.[42]

44

According to the opposition party, the official line from the current RMI administration is that they had no choice. At the least, many say, the RMI negotiators should have held Kwajalein hostage knowing how valuable star wars technology is to the U.S. Instead, not only did the RMI negotiating team concede Kwajalein in the rushed negotiations but it in effect allowed the U.S. to walk away from its obligations while holding RMI to its own.

> Compact II stripped everything that was of benefit to us, leaving only a long term American interest in Kwajalein. Like excusing the U.S. of its obligation to clean up its radioactive waste and provide medical care to our sick people, it was criminal.
> ...Marshallese Senator.

It's a shame the American legal system cannot carry the potency of such a base moral argument:

> We know that in the future our children are going to have thyroid problems, have cancer and all that, because if we're going back to Rongelap and it's still contaminated then our children is going to be hurt for life forever, for ages to ages. As the coconut crabs pass on their radiation to their small crabs for years and years (because of the oil in the coconut crabs), so will we. It's just like us, the radiation is going to be

in them, in their bodies, because we drank the water at that time of Bravo and it's still there and we've passed it on our children and their children. That is why we struggle for the 177.

...61-year-old Rongelapese woman.

Their backs may be against the wall but their history of surviving the straight ruin laid out for them by the U.S. says something. They don't break easily.

Birds That Eat Grainlessness

On the Federated States of Micronesia

The Federated States of Micronesia (FSM), like the RMI, gained independence in 1986 with the signing of its Compact of Free Association (Compact I) with the United States. With near identical terms as the Compact agreement between the RMI and the U.S., the FSM's Compact I provides that the U.S. is responsible for the defense of the FSM and the management of its foreign affairs. By all accounts, Compact I was a dismal failure, as the FSM has been unable to develop in any sustainable or self-sufficient way. In fact, U.S. aid makes up almost the entire domestic budget of the FSM. Irritated at this lack of growth, the U.S. under Compact II sternly dictates how the FSM can spend Compact II money and, much more importantly, sorely ignores the fact that when Compact II ends, the FSM will still be without a working political economy of its own because import models of development are not working in the FSM.

Now they're trying to tighten us under the new Compact, to make up for the failure of the last one...I don't know. There was a story told to me once. There was a guy who went somewhere in a village and he fell into a ditch. He kept yelling but nobody came. He had no choice but to eat and live off of what was in the ditch. He survived by just eating whatever was there and he stopped asking for help. Got to the point where people came and found him and tried to pull him out and he told them no. He got so used to his condition so that what was grotesque became normal and desirable. I'm not saying that we have actually normalized this and have no way of commenting on what's coming at us. My fear is that we might get too used to it. That's when you stop asking questions. You just take what's coming at you.
...42-year-old Chuukese man.

In 2007, the Federated States of Micronesia, which includes

Kosrae, Pohnpei, Chuuk, Yap, and all the smaller islands around these four main states, are being emptied of their people. FSM folks are trading in their taro, breadfruit and fish for canned meats, rice, and a chance to make it in the promised land. They are leaving their economically depressed homelands for the good life of Blue Collar America, many believing that something is seriously wrong with their islands and themselves. But they shouldn't beat themselves up. It's hard to smash ancient civilizations to make them fit into cans of Spam, Corned Beef and Western Economic Theories of Development.

> The real situation in FSM is that there was no development under Compact I. So, now the U.S. is sitting on us. Sitting on people and peering over their shoulder. The U.S. was disappointed that the islands didn't do more. But how much can you really expect people to do? You can't work miracles. If you're resource poor, you're resource poor. If oil prices are going up and you're trying to develop a mass tourist industry, what are you going to do? If you happen to be positioned here in the FSM, another fifteen hundred miles further than the prime tourist destination of Guam, that's an added disadvantage. I find myself critical of the U.S.' inability to understand this but I am also critical of people here. There's enough blame to go around. I'm ashamed of what's going on now. We're at a point where the conversation has just stopped. I think it'd be good if the U.S. just listen a bit.
> ...68-year-old man in Pohnpei.

The same man goes on:

> More and more people are picking up and leaving.
> That's why our migration rate is equal to our natural
> growth rate. Our NGR is around 2.1% per year and
> our emigration rate is very, very close to 2%. What
> this means is that we're in a no growth situation.
> Perhaps we're going to find out soon we're in a net
> loss situation as far as population goes. We figure
> that there are now 30,000 people from FSM living in
> the U.S. as of 2005. 20,000 Marshallese. Maybe
> about 10,000 Palauans. Maybe one out of every four
> Micronesians are living abroad now. There comes a
> certain point where local people say this is as far as I
> can go. This guy is clearly not going to budge. So
> screw it. I'll take what I can get and run. And I think
> that's a position that a lot of people find themselves
> in with respect to the U.S. now. You know, thinking
> it's hopeless to engage in this game of trying to move
> him over. That's bad but I think that's a calculation
> people make. I think it's happening now.

One 28-year-old Ponapean woman shares her thoughts on the
matter:

> I think people know that there's not really much we
> can do. We don't really have any other source of
> income, revenue, besides fisheries licenses. We don't

have much to export. We are import based. Majority of everything we consume here is imported. There's not much we can do about it. The people? There are not many opportunities for them. The U.S. military is something they can utilize to better themselves. They can go and make something of not having much out here. They send back money for their families. They travel, they get to see the world. A lot of them are trying to get their degrees while in the service. I try to encourage them to do that so they have more opportunities when they come back here.

But the real story here is not that the economies of the FSM are miserable, but rather, that this young government has arrived exactly where it was supposed to. Destination Desperation. In a deeply sad way, the people of FSM are living today at the last point on the Solomon trajectory. They are so economically dependent, so imprisoned by imports, so *desperate*, that they cannot even imagine another arrangement. This is their cancer: they are living at the edge of their imaginations, looking down. The physical result of this has been a retreat to service in the U.S. armed forces in record numbers. In 2007, so many young people are joining the military not out of volition but out of virulent hopelessness. Two Kosraean legislators comment:

We are at a disadvantage. Many of our people feel that joining the military is the option that is best for them because there is no other means of supporting their families. Other than the government (there are very few jobs in the private sector), there's no industry. Businesses are barely making it. The minimum wage here is $1.50. It's difficult to make it on that. Some people, although they want a different standard, they can't. We're under the poverty line. Right now, gas price is between $3.65 and $4 dollars. Everything has been going up while the salary has stayed stagnant. Unemployment is a big problem as well as U.S. pressure to downsize our government, which we can't do. The other way is to build more industries but that has not panned out. There have been summits on how best to fix this problem and of course everybody is saying the best way to do this is to build up the private sector, but the question is how to do that. In past economic summits, ideas were thrown around, but tourism comes with its own problems and fisheries has not panned out for the nation because we've started a lot of ventures that have just collapsed—the market, the management, the fish stock. We've tried this. Even agriculture hasn't worked out. Our farmers want to see a market where they can sell their goods at a price they want but it doesn't work like that. When they want to sell the products off island, there's no transportation, no reliable shipping. The airline is monopolizing. Continental has a monopoly. If we compare the airfare, there's a big difference. These are some of the problems of being such a small and isolated island with few people and little capital. Businesses look at volume and where they can make the most money.

We were just at the high school graduation and they were saying that 40% of the kids have been accepted into the college. We know from what we've seen that not all of them will come back with a bachelor's degree. It's rare. A lot of kids have gone up to college. What happens is when they get there, opportunities surround them everywhere. So they stay there and work. Working takes preference over going to school. Flipping hamburgers, cutting chicken, washing toilets. Those kinds of things. So I was clapping when they mentioned that but in the back of my head, I kind of tempered my clapping because I want to see these people come back with degrees, working.

Twenty five of the kids passed the [ASVAB] test last month and they're all going. Some of them have already left. Some of them are waiting for their departure date. They say that Kosrae, this year, has the most per capita that passed the military test.

Last month's numbers from the College of Micronesia (COM) entrance exam provide a snapshot of how young people from the FSM are doing. In Chuuk, for instance, only 1% was allowed entrance. [43] One 42-year-old Chuukese educator shares:

> 70% of our students here are remedial within a remedial program. We have to redo our curriculum because the current remedial curriculum is not even being passed. That's the reality of it. I mean, we administered a college entry test last month for the Chuuk high schools. Five out of 300 people passed. That's the regular program. It's a slightly bigger number for the remedial program. Most of them will end up in the remedial, remedial program. There's a big number of them that will not make it here.

The same educator reflects:

> Education here has not been good. I'm sure you've seen the videos and the reports. It was never properly designed or thoroughly thought out. The design of the education system in Micronesia is one that reflects an American school. It was something that was based on U.S. funding and continues to survive on U.S. funding, so that coupled with the fact that it was a system that was never built from the ground up to

reflect the need of the local people, it becomes a challenge to make it successful. Therefore, you have isolated success. The public schools here suffer from the funding shortages of the State although it tries to be an independent system. It still suffers from political interference and growing apathy among the staff. Teachers haven't had a pay raise since the 70s. You still have teachers paid the same they were in the 70s. And you wonder why you have a hard time keeping teachers. It gives attraction to other things.

On why youth are joining the military en masse, he says:

Young men and women are provided an opportunity to go off and serve in the military with the promise of having some assistance for school, and picking up skills while they're there, unfortunately they never accounted for going off and getting killed. The popular media that makes its way here, it glorifies war and violence. That coupled with the fact that some serious economic and health situations exist here make people leave. It has gotten to the point where there is very little else that moves here.

You want a good education? Good health? Not here. Try somewhere else. At the college here, we're trying to pick up the population who aren't able to make it anywhere else. We're not able to convince young people that it's worth trying hard in school. Because they've seen. It's almost like they're discouraged everywhere they look. It's easy for young people at an impressionable age to feel discouraged. The group we get here are the students who cannot go to college anywhere else. We would like to move to giving quality education—the same kind you can get outside the island—here. But it's not.

I've been in this for ten years. I got out of grad school in Hawaii and came directly here. Mostly I was trying to look for ways to support a more appropriate curriculum, in history, social studies. It became more an attractive side show than anything else. It's something good, people like to hear about their history, but if you can't nail it down to anything practical, then it doesn't work. It's hard for people to make connections. We can convince them but then when they step out of the classroom, they step right into the world we are in—Chuuk. It's pretty hard to talk history when people have no opportunities.

Other educators weigh in on this war for young people's imaginations:

Now I'm having a hard time trying to stop students from only thinking about joining the military after graduating from high school because the possibilities of not having enough money for college because the financial aid has been taken away and the scholarships are hard to get. It's giving them a slim chance to even think about going to college.

…Upward Bound Counselor, Kosrae.

Our main issue here is finances. The average salary on the island is about $7,000. So, for school, nobody can afford to go to school without the [federal Pell grant]. We're hearing it may be cut off. And schools in Hawaii last year tripled their tuition for Micronesian students. It was like a 150 percent hike. And most of the students found out about it after they got there. We had a large number of students who anecdotally I heard dropped out. And really the military is their best option they think. Last year, we lost number two, number three, number five, dropping out of UH Hilo. If you come first or second, the government provides a 75% scholarship. Number two just came from a dirt poor family. Anything less than a 100% scholarship, she wasn't going to be able to stay. I heard she joined the military. Our number three student—he joined the military right out of high school. I think our number five student—we heard he dropped out. Same reason. Couldn't afford tuition. Joined the military. That's what we're hearing. We have no reason to disbelieve it.

…42-year old administrator, Kosrae.

The [UH] tuition increase just massacred us. If we lose that Pell grant, that's everything. Every FSM student qualifies for the PELL grant, which is about $5,000 a year. You qualify for it if you are below a certain income. 100% of our parents are. And that's also what keeps the College of Micronesia (COM) alive and all its state branches. If we lose it, not only do we lose their main scholarship, but these schools have to close down. I don't see any way they can continue to exist without it. Every couple years we hear about it but it sounds like this year is more serious. Their big issue is that they're not getting a return for their money. Since 1987, we in Kosrae have had more than 2,000 graduates. Of these, we have maybe 18 who have gotten their BA degrees. That's less than one percent. So they have some 99.2% chance of not getting their degree.

...Principal, Kosrae High School.

Former FSM President, now at the COM-Pohnpei campus, shares his thoughts about Micronesian youth joining the military and the current war:

That's the problem with our kids, entering the war without really understanding what it is. Someone should talk to them about these things, about life insurance. This is serious stuff. To them, it's an adventure, and earning some money on this

58

incredible voyage of adventure. That's why they sign up for it. Then when they enter into the military, indoctrination takes over and then they become Superman, you know? Okay, I'm going to go out and save the world and that's why I am here. You talk to some of these Micronesian veterans. They have that attitude: we're out to save the world. Otherwise, we won't enjoy this democracy. Our freedom—you guys are enjoying freedom, because we're out there to protect it. That's indoctrination by the military. It's a bunch on nonsense.

In FSM, if you have to take a poll now, I'd say it's overwhelming support for the war and for our kids to go in. But I think that support is slowly eroding as more people are opening their mind. The dead are coming back. Several days ago, another Chuukese died in Iraq. So people are talking about it. But then, what the U.S. is doing here, is also sort of slowing down the anti-war sentiment, against Micronesians joining the armed forces. What the U.S. is doing here is they're using this federal program. For example, the farmers home. You take a loan out for a farmer's home. Now if you're just a regular FSM citizen, you submit your application for a loan to build a house, your application is not going to be a priority. It's a federal program but they're applying it not on equal basis now. So, if you're a FSM citizen and a veteran, you get top consideration, priority consideration. That's encouraging these families here to push their kids to go, saying: 'you go, you go. We want to build a nice house.' Another example is the life insurance they get. Now it's, what, $250,000? One Ponapean got four boys. They're not doing anything. They're high school dropouts. They were just staying home and drink and drink and he would wonder out loud, saying that, all four of my kids should go join the U.S. military, because if they die then I get more for them than if they were alive staying with me. That's four. That's one million dollars. So that's another attraction for Micronesian families to push their kids. Another thing the U.S. government is doing here is, you know…the veterans. I see them as kind of a fifth column through FSM. They're very organized through the U.S. embassy. Memorial Day, Veterans Day they have party, even U.S. Independence Day. They have become a very powerful force in FSM. They are wielding a very dangerous power in FSM. These are older men. Duty, honor, and country.

He continues:

I wrote an article about the Soram boy in *Pacific Magazine*. I saw, I think it was Soram's mother at the funeral. I saw it on t.v. The military guy walked up to her with a very smart, snappy salute, handed the flag to her, she walked back a little bit then he walked back a little bit, saying: 'honor, duty, and country.' I wondered if that woman knows what those words mean. I mean, to her, it doesn't mean anything.

Putting it plainly, he says:

> Did you visit the father of Skipper Soram? That's the effect of the war.

He speaks of the man who is now near comatose, lying on the floor of his house in rural Pohnpei. He suffered a stroke after his son's funeral and is not able to walk or talk. Not even to tell his pleading wife what it is he needs. He just lays there, grief a blanket around him. To be correct, the air around the Soram house is thick with mourning. Skipper Soram, the first Ponapean boy to die in Iraq, left behind a twin brother. A wind blows right through him.

Down that dirt road, another Ponapean family is trying to hold their home up, another father is dying another kind of death. One man, whose 25-year-old son survived an attack on his unit in Iraq, shares:

> Our son, since he's been hurt, has shut down. Shies away from interviews. The other day they had a graduation and they dedicated the yearbook to him.

They asked him to come but he said 'no.' He's sad. It will be a while for him. We don't force him.

The Soram boy was the first Ponapean to die in the war. Lives on the same road as us. Maybe five minutes away. His grandmother and my wife's mother were adopted at the same time, have the same root. He graduated from high school in 2000. Our son passed the ASVAB when he was a junior. That time when he joined, we were really in bad shape. We were suffering a lot. I was not working. I asked him if he wanted to college, but he said no, that he wanted to join the military to help us, and that he'd make use of the GI bill later to go to school. The military gave him a bonus, $12,000 dollars, when he enrolled. As far as helping us, he set up an account where we could access through the ATM, and he'd put money when he had change.

For this young man, life now is a struggle of spirit:

After four months, they gave him prosthetic legs and after a while he was able to walk with crutches. But he prefers the wheelchair. He cannot use the crutches on our road where we live. It needs to be on a smooth surface, a paved road. He has a power chair. He takes it, as he says, day by day. I hope he gets out of the worst stage, the recluse stage. We were told by experts that he'll get out of this stage. We're working on it with him. Right now, he can't be alone, can't be by himself. But being with family and friends is helping him keep his spirits high. We have five kids. It's hardest on the oldest one, his older brother. He was also in Iraq at the time, only a few miles apart. He's home now. He doesn't say much. He gets upset with other people with the slightest mention of his brother. The nine year old also, his youngest brother. They're very close.

The tragedy, as these things go, threw him into the spotlight. His parents say:

His biggest contribution was to our Compact, in 2003. When he was in intensive care, the U.S. Congress was having meetings in DC and people from the Department of Interior, the Assistant Secretary, mentioned him. The House passed our Compact unanimously. President Bush came and saw him also, visited several times, mentioned him in one of his speeches. He invited him to the White House for breakfast. I went with him. We got to meet with a lot of important people. The military, congress, private people. Even the rich man from Texas, one of the billionaires.

When asked by a reporter about why he wanted to join, the teenager said: to see something new, to help people, to help my parents. His father speaks to this:

> I cannot make a judgment about the war. I cannot see beyond his injuries. I personally feel liable because if we were in better shape then he wouldn't have decided to join the military. Somehow I have to tell him this before I die. I have to tell him that.

> The doctors, modern medicine, said he won't survive this. Doctors in Germany said he won't make it through the night. His kidneys were both shut down. His mother is from a strong clan, Lipitahn. That clan is known for being brave. They are one of the high clans. They got there through bravery. They say our son made it because he was Lipitahn. His mother's grandfather was one of the kings of Matellenium. High king. People say he's got the Lipitahn blood and royal blood. Our son takes strength from both sides, his mother's side and my father's side. My grandfather is a navigator, open sea navigator. Came from the outer islands of Chuuk, from Lukunor.

In Pohnpei, seat of the FSM national government, there's a flurry to find the true number of local people currently serving in the U.S. military. As one Ponapean Foreign Affairs officer says:

> We have very high ratios of people here serving in the military. We've been trying to get rates for the longest time. [The U.S. Department of Defense] is citing the Privacy Act. We have this meeting every year called the joint committee meeting where we get together with the U.S. government and talk about military issues. If we have anything we want to raise with them, one of them is the Guam military buildup. They just give updates and stuff. This next one is next month and they're supposed to give us some numbers, with a breakdown from each of the four [FSM] states. The number of people in the service we don't have. I don't know if they have it either. The number of people who enlist from here annually is about, I'd say, in the 20s or 30s a year. It's pretty high. And that's only from here. Not including the ones who enlist in Guam, Hawaii, the CNMI. So I'm sure it's much higher than that.

One 57-year-old Yapese educator makes a suggestion:

> The U.S. is not going to give [the official number of FSM citizens serving in the U.S. armed forces] as long as it's to their advantage to keep it secret. What the [FSM] national government should have required

is that pre-signing up, any FSM citizen who is going to volunteer for the U.S. armed forces, should sign up so we know exactly who's going in the military. And then after they discharge they should come back and sign out.

The same man shares another phenomenon:

Several kids here who decided to run away from their unit and come back here later tried to get back to the U.S., were picked up and thrown in jail. Several kids from the FSM were picked up in the immigration office and thrown in jail as deserters. I think they're still in jail. One of my friends told me there's a kid still in jail in Hawaii. They return home because one of their parents got sick and they decide not to go back. That's typical Micronesian attitude—to them it is a job and they think: I'm not going to go back to that job. They don't know what they've really signed to serve in the armed forces.

He shares another story, perhaps the best illustration of how war eats people:

There was a veteran from Woleai, an outer island of Yap. He's totally crazy now but he couldn't get VA help. He's crazy. His mind is gone. They say he's marching, you know, he uses the coconut leaves as

66

his gun. He pretends it's a gun and he marches from one end of the island to the other end, on the beach, shouting out 'order' in military jargon.

And this poor guy, he's not receiving anything. He's not a U.S. citizen. He doesn't have money to go back and seek assistance from the VA hospitals in the U.S. or Hawaii. They come out here, they don't get any benefit. Some of them tell me it's difficult to get benefits. When we are in the U.S., we are non-immigrants. We can stay, find jobs.

If Eating Folks is one half of the tale, the other is surely Exodus.

People may be leaving for the U.S. but, you see, not everyone goes to the US and succeeds. Only few of them. Some of them I heard, and nobody has done in-depth studies on it, some of them have join criminal gangs. Some of them have become homeless. But if they stay out here, they won't be homeless. They can always find homes, with their aunties, with their uncles, with their relatives. They won't go hungry. They don't need to go and eat in homeless shelters. They can always go and fish and get food from the land. You know, if I had my own way I would amend that Compact and not allow our kids to go to the U.S.

If you go to Chuuk, the villages are completely empty. They're ghost villages. They're in Guam.

What they're chasing is not even the American dream to be rich, but what they are chasing is welfare. They're chasing welfare in the U.S. The old and the young and the uneducated. The call from the U.S. is give me your old, your young, your uneducated, to come here and be on welfare.

...57-year-old Yapese man

Illustrating how people have come to be so economically dependent, he continues:

When I was in Guam once, we had a meeting and this guy from Chuuk, maybe 57 years old, he was pleading with the church organization in Guam, saying 'please pay for my power, my apartment, my family to stay in Guam. We cannot go back to Chuuk. If we go back to Chuuk we're all going to die.' I asked him when he came to Guam, he said four years ago. And I asked him how old he is now and he said 57. I said: 'Okay, you spent all of those 53 years living in Chuuk and you didn't die. Now, you're going to die?' He said: 'we have nothing, we have nothing in Chuuk.' I told him: 'what do you mean you have nothing? You have fish, of course the fish don't just jump to you. You have taro, you have breadfruit.' You know what he says? 'I like it here because I can just get the welfare check and go to the store and get what I need.'

The system is not working out. There are some people who really make an effort to stay in the U.S. and not become a burden. But then you have those who go there and only become a burden on the US welfare system.

One Chuukese woman, 47, could steal your heart with the fierceness of her clarity.

In telling a story about an encounter with an American about the state of fisheries in Chuuk, she slams a hammer on the nail of the U.S.-FSM relationship.

> One time I met this [National Oceanic and Atmospheric Administration], NOAA, guy whose job was to monitor the [Economic Exclusive Zone], EEZ. We met in Guam because he was stationed there. I didn't know what he really did for a living until we met up again here in Chuuk and he told me and I got pissed to the max and he wanted to shoot me. He was telling me what they do to catch the bad guys – the other guys who fish in our zone without permits. So we started talking about the fishing industry here and that's the time we had two boats. I started asking him

questions about the fishing industry. I was asking him how much Chuuk gets from the fishing industry and he was telling me there's an organization responsible for the fishing license, so a Taiwan ship would come in and want to fish in the zone and they would buy a fishing license, which is maybe a couple thousand dollars. For example, Taiwan will come, pay a small fee, and take the fish and sell it. And that's it. They will fish and leave. So, the ship would come in and fish in the zone, and load up with, say, 900 tons of fish. On the market that will probably net at least half a million dollars. Compared to that lousy fee to fish.

I asked him: 'does that make sense to you? Economical sense?' I said 'fuck you. You know what's wrong with you. You know why these people are so screwed up? Because you bring your million dollar shit and it's like you just give them a knife and say: 'here, you kill yourself' instead of saying 'this knife is dangerous. This is how we use it.' And you teach them how to use that knife instead of just giving it to them and expecting them to figure out how to use it.

Anybody who wants to fish in the zone pays the licensing fee to the FSM and then they can fish anywhere in the FSM waters. My issue was that these people have no idea how to set up the industry to reap maximum benefit from it. The U.S. could have shown them how to reap maximum benefits. Instead, all they do is just monitor. The Taiwanese and the Chinese is reaping maximum benefits whereas us, all we have is the licensing fees worth maybe $30,000. In one year, these ships can make 12 million dollars easy and we only had $30,000 in fees. Nobody here seems to conceptualize that. They're depleting your resources and your island is fucked up. It's like [and she points to the food on her plate] I give you more and I just eat a little bit. It's like I would rather feed all of you. Give you all my food. And starve.

The same woman speaks about a kind of cultural warfare alive and well in the islands:

The culture is losing its force. Right now, half of the culture in Chuuk is copycat of the U.S. They think the U.S. culture is the greatest. I was at a wedding here. My nephew was getting married but it was a U.S. wedding. Afterwards I went up to the mother and told her that she didn't know how to put on a U.S. wedding. I asked her why she had her sister sit at her place of honor beside the newlyweds. She said because her sister was married to the Vice President of the nation and that she wanted everybody to know we adore her and respect her. I told her she didn't realize that that seat was hers because she brought her

71

son up, raised him as a single mom, that that was her honor, that you put honored guests at that table, not just anybody.

Here's the problem: we want to mimic the U.S. culture and we just screw it up. It's like I want to copy how you make coffee but I don't know all the ingredients. I just taste it, like it, and now I'm trying to make it but it will never happen because I don't have the recipe. I don't own that recipe. A lot of the things that are happening here, when I see it, I am so pissed off and I am more sad. They think it's cool. They think that when you perform a wedding, for example, and it's not the traditional wedding, they think: 'wow, it's cool.' When you host a party and it's not a traditional style party, they think it's cool. Here, they have a perverse idea about that.

Going straight to the root—education—she shares a theory. And it stings.

The youth of Chuuk these days are totally lost. The more I leave Chuuk and observe it from afar, and then when I come back, there's a bigger gap between the generations. Since Compact I until now, I think the reason why they haven't been able to bring up the education standard to a level where we can look at it and be proud of it is that they know: it is very easy to manipulate uneducated people. Very easy. That's my conclusion.

You can manipulate uneducated people, telling them exactly what you want them to believe. If you tell them you can catch a fish just with your teeth, they will believe it.

There are people in the government who pull strings and have their way done at all cost. Local elections prove that. I remember these two guys. One graduated only from elementary. One finished one year at the Guam Community College, and then he advertised here that he got his B.S. from GCC. Do you get a bachelor's degree from GCC? I don't think so. Here in Chuuk, you can literally buy votes. I remember, the day before an election, the power was out, and people were out with flashlights buying, selling votes. Especially the youth, they cannot independently think. There are more dropouts here in Chuuk than anywhere else in the country. You can count the people with bachelors and masters and doctorates here in Chuuk. You can count them on your fingers. And we're the most populated [island in the FSM].

I ran for office once and lost. This guy told me that I should run again and this time buy votes. And I said why? He said because I was one of the smartest women in Chuuk but that there were more stupid people than smart people in Chuuk.

In Pohnpei, one 57-year-old man describes the U.S.-FSM relationship in three sentences.

> People worship the U.S. here. It's scary. Like last election for our President, I heard in casual conversation that we shouldn't have this guy because the U.S. government doesn't like him.

Another 68-year-old man in Pohnpei puts it this way:

> It's not enough for Condoleeza Rice to say this is the Year of the Pacific and let's all be friends now. Because in a hundred different ways, that's not the message that's being given, any more than it's the message begin given in the middle east. No. The message is: To the extent that you can help us help ourselves—to that extent—we'll continue to graciously assist you. That's not American democracy. It's death.

In the thirteenth century, a Sufi wrote something exquisite in both its beauty and sadness:

How wonderful it was to be for a while with those who surrender. Others only turn their faces one way, then another, like pigeons in flight. I have known pigeons that fly in a nowhere, and birds that eat grainlessness, and tailors who sew beautiful clothes by tearing them to pieces.[44]

Today, the birds are singing a song of separation. Of mourning. For a world on its way out.

Looking back, one man says:

> I think what we did under the Compact was we tried to develop our islands sort of from top down. We should have done it the other way. You know, in the village—slow development of the villages, up. Maybe approach it in such a way that those who are depending on subsistence living, to enhance their subsistence living. I think that would have been better than what we did in the 1980s.

And there it is. A piece of the old wisdom floating to the top.

Here's another:

> You know I keep thinking about this. I don't know if this is why they're trying to give us hard time to give

out the money. They always say that Chuuk misusing, misuse money. And they're giving us hard time. Maybe because Chuuk is the most place that we fighting against the Americans. We don't want them just to come from outside and set up their business in Chuuk. Those are the kind of things we're trying to protect our people from. We learn lessons from Guamanians, from our neighbor island Guam and our friends in Hawaii because now, no more Hawaiian, no more Chamorus.

...69-year-old Chuukese woman

The same woman talks of another combat zone:

It's true, especially people on this island [Weno, the urban center of Chuuk]. They think that good food is from the store. The rice and meat. Not breadfruit and fish. Now we have hard time teaching them that local food is good for them, better for their health. It's hard now-a-days to go back to the old ways. These kids, they've grown up with rice; they believe in rice.

If these people are going to make it, they're going to need to throw out the rice as well as the god.

The land—where just last year 80% of the women seeking prenatal care at Public Health were anemic—has had enough Death By Import.[45]

A Dream With Fight In It

On Belau

The Republic of Palau (Belau), an island nation that until recently held the title of the newest country in the world, gained its independence in 1994 when its Compact of Free Association with the U.S. came into force. Belau was the last of the former Trust Territory islands to gain independence because the U.S. disapproved of the anti-nuclear clause in Belau's Constitution, which in 1981 was celebrated as the world's first nuclear-free Constitution. After more than a decade of grassroots struggle to preserve the anti-nuclear provision, the U.S. desire to be able to transit nuclear material through Belau proved too potent, and an option for militarization in favor of the U.S. remains. As an independent country, Belau conducts its own foreign affairs. Under Compact I, the U.S. remains responsible for Belau's defense for 50 years. Today, as the U.S. turns its attention to expanding its military presence in Guam, Belau is being eyed, deliciously, as the site of R & R for U.S. soldiers who may need to leave Guam every once in a while to stretch their legs and, likely, future military exercises. At the time of this writing, the Republic of Palau is set to re-negotiate its Compact of Free Association with the U.S.

79

Two narratives have gripped Belau. One of beauty. One of blankness. The young are telling the latter. Like their cousins throughout Micronesia, Palauan teenagers are becoming economic conscripts in the current war on terror. Last month (June 2007), dozens signed up. Stepping up as the common denominator for the move were the usual suspects: the economy, education, adventure, patriotism, freedom. Boredom. But for many, motivation had nothing to do with it. Some just bumped, if you will, into it.

> Actually I didn't really think much about it. I was just roaming around Palau Community College seeing some friends and one of my friends said: 'Hey, let's go take the test.' So I did. Then they called me and told me I passed. It took me like a year and a half to think about it. I wasn't sure if I could even make it. Then I pulled myself together and thought I might as well.
>
> ...24-year-old Palauan female.

> It was like a bet. It was four of us, me and three of the boys. It was not my intention to go to the military. We just went and everybody failed except me and my best friend. We were like brother and sister in school. I was supposed to go to Hilo, Hawaii for school. Two weeks later they called me and told me I passed the

test. I said: 'Okay.' But it was not my intention to go. I was going to go to Hawaii. I even got the acceptance letter. I got in. But I went to my recruiter and showed it to him, but he said I already swore in and I could not get out. He said: 'No.' I said: 'Okay, fine.' So I just called my mom and said nevermind and told the school: 'Thank you for accepting me but I cannot come. Something came up and I have to go.' They told me that if I don't go, I was going to go to jail, because I had sworn in. So my mom and dad went to sign the paper because I was still 17. Now, sometimes I regret it.

...Another 24-year-old Palauan female.

When the recruiters came, the teacher told us that if we were going to take the military exam, we were free for the whole day and we didn't have to come back to class. So we went over there and took the test. All six of us took the test so we could get off early. We were already planning to go to one of the parks to hang out and relax after class. When I was taking it, I could've done better on the ASVAB, but I was just messing around so I could get out of class for the rest of the day. Next thing you know our names were coming out of the radio stations, of people passing, and we freaked out. Actually, I missed it on the radio but they also posted it on the bulletin board outside of the Palau Community

81

College and my brother was taking classes there and he read my name among the people who passed the test. And people were coming up to me and congratulating me for passing the test. And then, because I passed the test, my parents just let me.

…29-year-old Palauan male.

The same Palauan male speaks about his experience of the recruiting process:

They told us that after basic training and advanced individual training, we would get like 30 days paid vacation wherever you want. That's one thing that got us. Me and my cousin thought we'd go see Paris. France or whatever. Actually, they only give you 30 days, but it's not really leave. It has got to be like emergency to leave. They only gave us two weeks and two weeks is not enough to fly from the states to here. You lose maybe like 2-3 days just to get here. When you join you have zero leave, so you earn it. So after basic and [Advanced Individual Training], AIT, you can't use the 30 days yet, not really, unless it's an emergency.

Like when the recruiter asks you what kind of [Military Occupational Specialty], MOS, you want, what kind of work you want. I just said I wanted something fun. They told me I was going to be a field artillery surveyor, the one to work inside a warehouse and be the one doing inventory and counting all the ammunition that goes in and out, but that's not what I was going to be doing. When I got there I was surveying the artillery, the big cannons, even the small ones, the motors. We use this machine kind of like a GPS. We give them the area coordinates and an angle they're shooting at, and they use that to fire the cannons. So that's what I was doing. At first it was hell because you can't sleep. You'd be right there with the cannons so every time they fire you wake up. But then you got used to do it. After awhile, it was like nothing. It's funny when the new recruits come and we see them try to sleep and then boom and they wake up and freak out. It's funny but after awhile it gets boring. Every day you train, just to prepare you if something breaks out.

The fish can't be blamed for biting. With dim to desperate economic prospects throughout Micronesia, island children can hardly be expected to fend off advances of U.S. military recruiters. Current recruitment into the U.S. military is highest in U.S. territories, where poverty has stolen the imagination of the youth, resulting in an outrageous over-representation in the U.S. armed forces. [46] It such disempowered climates, it is no wonder that island children snatch up offers of instant cash, *big* cash, like salvations.

Some can walk away with upwards of $80,000 in recruitment incentives. It's an attraction so easy to appreciate.

One 24-year-old Palauan female lends her voice to this issue:

> It was a whole lot of bullshit [the recruiters] gave me. They said I would be flying in planes, taking pictures of whatever we need to be printing. But that was just never true. And that's one thing that made me mad because I like planes. It was just so different from what they told me. They told me that we'd be busy all the time, printing out stuff, doing a lot of missions, but it's just not true. They make it sound great. They tell you that you can go wherever you want to go, whenever. But that wasn't true. Before you go to training, you got like a wish list of where you want to go and be stationed at, after all your training is done. If you lucky, they give you that place. If not, you got to deal with what they give you. I'm lucky I got Texas. But then a lot of people I talked to, it didn't happen for them.

> My squad leader told me that I should think about becoming a recruiter. I was like: 'hell no.' I ain't gonna tell no other Palauans that they should join the Army and end up being in the war and dying and their families be all frustrated. I don't want to do that.

I'll tell them to go to school, the Air Force, something.

The same girl goes on to share her experience trying to take classes while in active duty:

They don't really encourage us to take classes. They just tell you it's a good idea but when we start thinking about it, start applying for classes and all that, they just kind of push you away, tell you we got more important things to do. First time I got there, I told them I want to take classes either online or at the university. They said okay, they can do that. But then I started doing my paperwork, they were like: 'No, we don't have time. You can't go. You can't really take classes because we have a lot of missions we got to do' and I went: 'Okay.' And I just got there, so I was thinking we do. But then we never did anything. And then I kept bugging them about it, and they were like: 'No, you can't because the Commander doesn't want you to. The Commander doesn't want anybody to take classes.' He's the Commanding Officer in the unit. I don't know if he really said that, but that's what I was told.

Another 24-year-old Palauan female shares this story:

When we came back [from Afghanistan], we had to
see a psychiatrist. That's the rule. At night, I couldn't
sleep. If a little thing falls down, I jump up and look.
Over there, they say sleep like a cat. Don't sleep like
you're gone. Just like a cat nap so when something
happens, just get up and you're ready. Usually, we
sleep with BDUs, boots, gas mask, all our things,
using our bags, rucksacks as pillows. Once they say
'get up, get up,' you're out. At night, I had dreams.
When I get up I'm sweating. It's hot. Because I'm
still thinking I'm there, especially for the first two
weeks I got back. It was so hard because I couldn't
sleep. I just get up. Even if my roommate just moves
something, I get up and get mad. I was easy to get
mad. I'm thinking I'm still in that kind of life out
there even if I'm safe in my room. Now, it's better.
But to me, it was a good experience. I would do
anything to go back. Why? I'm not sure. Sometimes I
question myself. But still, half of me still wants to go.

The same girl tells an anecdote to communicate why some
who have gotten out, go back:

There was this guy from Guam. Santos was his last
name. He used to work with [us]. He was a reservist.
Then they got activated to go to Iraq. They were in

86

Iraq for almost one year. I'm telling you, when that guy got back he looked sick. I mean, he looked so sick. You're just talking to him and he's looking at you like 'who are you?' He's still confused. It's funny you ask me why I want to go back. I asked him that question. Because he changed from reserves to active duty. He said, I don't know but I would do anything to go back to Iraq. He said: 'I don't know but I want to go back.' You see, he resigned from work because he couldn't work. He was so short tempered to the [clients]. Even when they were talking nice to him, he'd turn around and get mad. Next thing you know, they're at it. So I guess he just decided to go back to active duty again. Last time I heard, he was stationed in Washington. A lot of them, they went back.

Speaking about the war, one young solider shares:

I don't believe in the war but there's nothing I can do about that. If they say I got to go, I got to go. But I don't put no pride in it. With the war, I don't know— I don't pay much attention to it. I don't agree with it. I don't understand why they always got to send a lot of us out there and then a lot of us come back in coffins and all that shit. They could find a way to stop it but then they're making it worse by sending more people out there. I don't know.

We just try to ignore it. A lot us that know each other
in the Army, whenever we come together—if we go
to church, play basketball, whatever activity we be
doing—we don't ever talk about it. We don't. We
don't talk about it. We don't find it important to us. I
also be surprised, like other people from the states,
they talk about it. Us, we don't. We don't talk about
it. We just talk about how we miss home, how we
know each other.

Such is the story the young are telling. Part of it at least.

The other—the one of beauty, the one old women tell best—
is what the rest of the region remembers as our Moment of
Might, when the people of Belau fought for more than a
decade for a nuclear-free Constitution. They waged a noble
struggle against enormous U.S. and local governmental
pressure to approve a Compact of Free Association
agreement favorable to the military interests of the U.S.,
which wanted to be able to transit nuclear weapons through
Belau. The story is beautiful but it is also bloody. Because
those who tell it do so with a heavy in their eyes, it is also
hard to hear. Two older Palauan women, 63 and 72, go back
and forth, weaving the story of the people's struggle to keep
Belau nuclear-free:

One of the sad things about this whole thing is that the few of us who were fighting were not only fighting the U.S., but also our government and our own people. Family members were fighting against each other. The struggle began in the mid '70s during the establishment of the Federated States of Micronesia (FSM) Constitution. In the referendum of 1978, Belau and the Marshall Islands did not ratify the FSM Constitution. After that, both Belau and the Marshall Islands had to establish their respective Constitutions. Now the Micronesian island block is divided into four entities: the CNMI, the FSM, the Marshall Islands, and Belau. In Belau, we were so eager to practice what we learned from the U.S. for so many years by putting the concepts and ideals of democracy and freedom into practice, and making political sovereignty a reality. It seemed right to do so. It still seems right. But it was not a good idea for the U.S. We assumed that what was good for the U.S. was good for us too. We were devastated when the U.S. Ambassador came to Belau and informed our Constitution framers that the U.S. didn't approve of the provision in our Constitution that prohibited the U.S. from transiting nuclear weapons in Belau. We ignored the U.S. demand and went ahead with the referendum. Our very own Constitution, our first one ever, was ratified with 92% in favor of it. There was pressure to revise the Constitution to get rid of the nuclear-free provision, but the revised version was never ratified. We went through a lot to reinstall the original Constitution. The unorganized group at the center of the fighting organized officially as an environmental group called *Kltal-Reng*. The environment became the main focus of our activities. Little did we know that in less than two years, we would take on an even bigger cause—to uphold our Constitution and keep U.S. militarism out.

The new government announced that a plebiscite on the Compact of Free Association (COFA) was to take place within two to three months. For almost two years after the establishment of the new local government, the first President would come by where we gathered during those long nights fighting for Belau. We were very close to him and would ask or discuss anything with him. When we asked him about the COFA, you could tell that he himself did not know what we were getting ourselves into. But he had faith that the U.S., as a big brother and strong nation, would not take advantage of our young and weak nation. As a result, nobody took the issue of the plebiscite seriously or cared to find out about the COFA. Why? First, we did not know what the COFA was. Only a handful of people in high positions in the Trust Territory Government had an inkling of what this thing was all about. The general public was

90

in the same boat as we were, and never heard of a COFA. Second, with our Constitution as the highest law of the land, what could go wrong? To us, our Constitution was our protector and defender. And third, the President who was elected by the pro-Constitution people did not see how the COFA could affect the Constitution, and therefore we were lax. There was no need to be up in arms. In fact, many people I knew said that the U.S. would be very proud to see an island they "saved and developed" become independent politically.

Our government organized a committee to conduct a political education campaign on the COFA throughout Belau. Meanwhile, *Kltal-Reng* took the initiative to educate our own members on the COFA. The more we learned about the document, the more we became convinced that Belau was heading into a deep, deep trouble. There were issues in the COFA that were incompatible with our two year old Constitution—and they were major issues! Yet our government and the U.S. government denied their existence. It also blew our minds to find out that the COFA was not a treaty, but instead a U.S. Law. And our heart sank when we realized that our chance to become independent politically might never become a reality. Noticing that the political educators were misinforming, lying and just outright forcing people

91

to vote "yes" for the COFA, *Kltal-Reng* members took it upon us to get the facts out to the ordinary people. Our main problems were: we were working against time because it took us almost two months to educate ourselves on the document; we did not have financial resources because most members were old men and women in their late 60s and 70s, and the development of materials was almost impossible. There was no place to print information except at government offices. That was a no-no. It was a very good excuse to get fired from the government. We worked in the hours between 5:00 p.m. and 7:30 a.m., which was just not enough to do all this and get out to the villages. To make things harder, there was no road around Babeldaob. Most of our travels were during the night and on weekends. Luckily, several senators (God bless them) gave us their boats to use, free. We donated money for gas, for transportation.

We did not barge into the villages and demand community meetings. We asked permission from appropriate people to visit certain people and families. It was most effective to meet with families. The incompatible issues between the COFA and our Constitution were pointed out in both documents. Luckily, the Constitution was still fresh in most people's minds. It was not until the third plebiscite that the Belau government changed its tactics and started harassing and pressuring people they thought were anti-COFA. *Kltal-Reng* was the only group educating people on the COFA besides the government's political education committee. There were several times when we were confronted by the government high officials at the community level. The officials would show up at villages where we would meet. They came to disrupt the meetings and to tell people that we were not telling the truth. First, they tried to be friendly, but later they became hostile and rude. With situations like this, we usually stepped back and gave them a chance to talk to the people. There were a few times when we were invited to join the meetings just to be ridiculed and made fun of. Little did they know that such actions back fired on them. As usual, the officials did not have facts and figures to support their position and gave information that was not true. They lied and pressured villagers to support their position—a pro-U.S. military position. As for us, we were always ready and prepared for such challenges. Our position was that we are Palauans who were concerned about the future of Belau. Even if the people decided to make Belau a military island, as long as they were informed, then we were satisfied—not happy, of course.

The government took stronger measures against *Kltal-Reng* members as well as anybody who they thought was anti-COFA. Individual members of *Kltal-Reng* were visited and warned not to go to the villages, and told to stop educating people. When it became too dangerous to go to the villages, we went at night. We traveled from village to village, through hill and forest, in the middle of the night just to meet with a few people. Boats would drop us and pick us up at night in designated areas. During the day, we would meet with women in the taro patches in order to keep them, and us, from getting into trouble. We met with small groups, individuals, and families to avoid attracting attention from the pro-COFA people. If villagers or church groups invited us, that's when we'd conduct big meetings and presentations. One of the best tactics we used was to pose questions to the villagers to answer and discuss. Deciding for themselves became the best approach, as long as they knew where the COFA conflicted with the Constitution. I can remember one village where the majority of the villagers were pro-COFA. During our presentation, the government groups came and took over the meeting. The villagers asked for a debate where they themselves would ask the questions and the two sides would take turns answering. At the next plebiscite, the majority of the voters in that village voted against the COFA. It turned out to be one of the best confrontations we got into.

How we were harassed and treated kept many of our relatives and co-workers at a distance. They were afraid to be seen and be associated with us on a daily basis, and especially during customary obligations. The customary obligations became strenuous. Many people we worked very hard with during the ratification of the original Constitution were now fighting against that Constitution. Government employees were the first people to jump to the other side because they had money to party and travel within and outside Belau.

When it became clearer that certain provisions in the COFA were incompatible with our Constitution, it became harder and harder for the government to entice people. Parties with lots of food and drinks became ineffective. The government ordered the schools to close so that teachers and students would go out campaigning for the COFA. The task of the students was to talk to their parents about their future. The meals for the sick at the hospital were terminated, and the prisoners were let loose. When these did not work, the electricity and the water were turned on and off at certain times. When all of these things still did not make a dent, the government closed its governmental operations—except for a few nurses and a bunch of policemen—and organized a furlough.

This was the climax. The year was 1987. The Legislature building became the furlough headquarters and camp site. There they slept, ate, conducted their harassment tactics, and watched X-rated films, day in and day out. They occupied the whole place with no respect at all. The furlough people organized teams to go out and harass individuals, families, villages, and institutions. Members would meet with people from their states, those living in the village and those living in Koror. A list was made of names of people to harass and kill. Some admitted that they picked their own mother's name, or sister's, or a very close relative, and did not have the nerve to harass and kill them. Electricity to supporters' homes was disconnected. Reconnection was almost impossible. My house was without electricity for almost three months. Individuals were visited and threatened by the furlough members to do what they were told. Or else. All 16 villages (states) were forced to send food. Government vehicles and gas were used as the government saw fit. Government employees had to go to the furlough camp to sign their name in order to get their paycheck. Members of the House of

Delegates were forced to sign a special referendum to lower the 75% requirement necessary to change the nuclear provision in the Constitution. The President's people blocked the entrance to my house with huge rocks. Ironically, guns were not allowed in Belau except for the policemen, yet furlough people tried shooting one man's house almost every night. The whole police force was with the furlough; some of them admitted that they were forced to do these things.

By this time, the supporters of the Constitution had increased. As a big group, we filed a class action lawsuit, which was later withdrawn by force. We, the women, resubmitted the lawsuit. The night before the court hearing, September 7, four things happened. The electricity all over Koror was turned off; a community building in Koror got burned down; a bomb exploded near Gabriella's house; and Mr. Bedor was shot at his son's office. He died the next day. The man was also a strong supporter of the Constitution. The furlough people went to the court with red things tied around their heads and a big van was covered in black with "Black September" written all over it. The van, we were told later, was going to be our casket.

Shortly after returning from the morgue, the policemen went to Mr. Bedor's house, demanding that the women who filed the lawsuit sign the paper to withdraw their name. They said that if they didn't sign their name by 4:00 p.m., they would come back and kill everyone with bombs. Many women were at this man's house because his granddaughter died two days before. The tension for the safety of the other women became unbearable and forced me to withdraw my name too.

It really hurts when someone you trusted all your life betrays your trust. And that's exactly what happened. Since the end of WWII, we Micronesians (Marshallese, Ponapeans, Chuukese, Kosraeans, Saipanese, Chamoru, Yapese, and Palauans) were told again and again that we would become politically independent once our protectorate, the U.S., develops our islands. For many years, we built our high hopes for this political independence. We looked up to the U.S. with every ounce of our trust. In fact, we would have given everything we had to the U.S. if only she asked openly and in an honest way. We looked up to the U.S. as our hero, not our colonizer.

We needed a chance to prove to ourselves, to prove that it is better to be the head of a mouse than the tail of a tiger.

One of them continues:

Once, when the school was closed, my friend and I went to school. Workers were on the street. They said: 'Come and join us.' Ignoring them, we went to the office. The principal stopped me from going to my classroom. He said that if I went to my classroom, they would bomb the place. I said: 'Okay. I'll just go and get my students' papers and do my work at home.' The government was going to fire all of us high school teachers. They closed the school and we didn't get our paychecks for a long time. In fact, we did not get paid for the whole summer.

We had families against each other. Like my relative, the wife of a local politician. She and another relative of mine were supporters of the Compact, while I was against it. One day they asked me to join them for dinner. So I went. They tried to convince me to support the Compact. I asked them: "Why?" They really did not know what was in the Compact. I said: 'You tell me. When your husband was not a politician, we were working together to save our original Constitution. I still remember. We were at your store trying to form our group to support the Constitution. We were very poor. We were eating tuna fish and tapioca, and we were happy. What happened? Why did you change? Why are you not supporting our Constitution? This Compact conflicts with our Constitution because of our nuclear free provision, and also because two-thirds of Babeldaob was to be reserved for U.S. military use. What's left for us?' These two ladies, older than me, just couldn't answer me. I continued: 'Tell me, what happened? Why change? We had a goal. Our goal was for the Constitution.' Because her husband became a politician, she had to support what the U.S. wanted. The other lady, whose husband was also a government leader, also supported the Compact.

One 57-year-old Palauan man reads from journal entries he made during that time:

The threats really began on August 6. I received a phone threat: 'If you continue with the case, we will firebomb your office.' The second threat was on August 13. The guy called at 2 o'clock and said that if we don't stop, they'll blow up the office. There were things in between. On September 3, I wrote: 'The situation is very tense. The police continue to threat as normal. The police were on the other side. The government furloughed.' The government applied pressures and said if the Compact was not passed, no payday. I was working here on September 4 when a government employee came to cut the power line to this office. I interfered and prevented him from cutting the power line. Then on September 5, while I was working, a relative called at 11 o'clock to report that a red car with a tinted window was shooting at the home of the Speaker of the House because he was anti-Compact. He and his wife and children may still be in the house. After the shooting, lights on the entire island got turned off. September 7—Gabriella and her niece came to the office to talk about the case which we were going to argue the next day at 2 o'clock. She was concerned about their safety and security. The situation had become very tense. In the evening at 10:30 p.m., the power was turned off all over the island. Simultaneously, a bomb exploded near Gabriella's house, a big building burned down, and the same red car came to the office and shot my father. Because the power was shut off, father had come back to the office to get his flash-light, which he left there. When the red car came, a man came to the door came looking for me. When father opened the door for him, he shot him three times and fled.

The 63-year-old woman goes on:

> We were so happy that the nuclear issue was included
> in our Constitution. Then we found out that the U.S.
> was really against it. The whole struggle has been
> going on for many years, and still very few people
> understood the Compact. It was a few of us who
> realized that we needed to keep Belau for us and
> needed to make hard decisions for ourselves, instead
> of giving our island—our rights, our children's
> future—to U.S. militarism. For many years, the U.N.
> reminded the U.S. that the time to terminate the
> Trusteeship was long overdue. However, in our
> minds, militarization was never an option as a
> replacement of the Trusteeship Agreement.

The 72-year-old woman continues:

> They were studying this Compact for a long time
> when I joined them. When I started reading it, I
> stopped so many times saying: 'Wait, wait. Why did
> these men sign this document?' Who signed it? My
> cousin. And he was supposed to be a smart man. I
> would not have done the same, knowing what it
> entailed. The government workers were just
> following the leaders. Only a handful of them read
> the document. Even people who were assigned to
> educate the public did not know what the Compact

102

said. We always referred to passages and pages in the two documents when we met with people to discuss the issues. The difference with the government educators and us is that they campaigned, and we educated.

The 63-year-old woman continues:

> With the Compact, our government leaders should have looked at how things were going to be for the long term. They did not realize that the U.S would be supporting us financially for only 15 years, with the amount of money declining drastically, while the power of the U.S. to use Belau for its militarism would continue for 50 years or more.

From the early '70s to the late '80s, U.S. political pressure was squeezing Palauan leadership and the latter was squeezing the people who opposed the Compact for want of a nuclear-free provision. In one U.N.-sanctioned referendum, 92% of the people approved the nuclear-free Constitution.[47] But it didn't stick. The 57-year-old Palauan man shares some of this history:

> We had a referendum on July 9, 1979, and 92% of the people approved our Constitution. The U.S. objected to the ratification of the Constitution. We

filed a lawsuit. The Trust Territory Court at that time was a creation of the Department of Interior (DOI). The judges were appointed by the DOI. They were employees of that Department. Despite the referendum being observed by the United Nations, the Trust Territory court ruled that the Constitution was null and void. The leadership of Belau, under U.S. pressure, amended the Constitution. They removed any provisions that could be offensive to U.S. military policy. The people rejected the amended Constitution by 80%. The people wanted the original Constitution. A year later, the original Constitution was put up for another referendum, and it was again ratified, this time by 81 or 82%.

He goes on:

Belau had three referendums for our Constitution. The FSM, only once. The Marshalls, only once. The CNMI, only once. We were all under the Trust Territory. We had the Compact negotiated between three entities. The U.S. allowed the Marshallese and the FSM to go through the referendum process only one time. But Belau? We had to do it about ten or eleven times until people got so tired.

According to him, one of the glaring problems of the Compact was that under it, if the U.S. wanted to use any private lands in Belau for military activities, all it had to do was 'notify' the government and, within 60 days, Belau was obligated to make that land available to the U.S. He says:

> In the U.S., you have to go through eminent domain proceedings to take land. Under the Compact, eminent domain did not apply. We are not U.S. citizens. That's why I said: 'No Way.' A lot of people misconstrued the women's position, my position, as anti-American. But the question was whether the Compact agreement incorporated the concept of free association, or instead, annexation. The concept of free association first sold to the people of Belau was a good one, but that concept changed to be more like a concept of annexation. To me, it was not free association. Once the government of the U.S. decides how much land it wants, the U.S. need only notify the government of Belau. The government of Belau "shall make" the desired land available. Thankfully, the appellate court ruled that our government cannot use eminent domain to take land to lease it to the U.S. because military usage of the land is not for the benefit of Belau, as required by our Constitution.

He shares an analogy:

> A man once told me: 'You know? The way I look at it is that this Compact of Free Association established

a business corporation. And our President and the members of the Congress are like the Board of Directors.' If you look at it, Belau has become a sovereign nation only when the U.S. needs a vote in the United Nations to support Israel. Belau always votes with the U.S. Belau and the FSM. We were the first ones to get into the war. That's the only time when we're sovereign nations. But when we sort of deviate from U.S. policy, we become a colony again.

Of course this Voting With the U.S. at the U.N. Thing is not unique to Belau. As one researcher at the Micronesian Seminar in Pohnpei puts it:

Micronesia? We always go with the U.S. at the U.N. 90, 95% of the time. That's the deal. [The island nations of Micronesia] get to be independent, and the U.S. expects them to support it. Not only the war but everything that comes up, like voting 'no' on things that condemn Israel. Peter Rosenblatt, under the Jimmy Carter administration, told me—we became good friends—he told me that Micronesia's missing out on its chance because the Jewish counsel in the U.S. would like to do something in thanks for its continual support for Israel on these things, you know, without even thinking about the question. The FSM Ambassador in Washington wasn't as much aware as he should've been about the opportunity here to pick up some spare change from the Zionists who were appreciative of FSM support.

Thankfully, cynicism has no staying power in Belau. Anyone who has seen her would know. Perhaps this is part of her majesty—that things profane may come to her but do not find the shelter they seek, perhaps because hers is the land where the Creator laid herself out to show off what she can do.

After more than a decade of plebiscites, struggle, and loss, folks are still hopeful and open to change. They are just tired.

> I thought that the '80s and '90s would be a nation building time. A time for the people of Belau to put aside their differences and seriously decide what was good for the future of Belau and how to get there.
> ...63-year-old Palauan woman

Tired but clear.

> I feel that the U.S. considers us garbage, or worse. If they could get rid of us, they would do so, so they can use this island as they please. It is scary to know that military build-up in Guam has started. Some Guamanians are saying that they cannot survive without the U.S. But, if we all get together and really

look at what we have, what we need and the kind of life we want to build, we can all survive.

Another Palauan woman, 51, thinking about the near future, looks forward:

> Our leadership has invited the U.S. military from Guam to Belau for R & R. Our Compact gave them the option to extend the airport. Two months ago, the Navy Commander went with our Vice President, because our Vice President was a Colonel in the U.S. Army, he was stationed in Kwajalein before—they went to Anguar and they say they will expand the airport for the commercial plane to come. But is that really true? Maybe not commercial but maybe some military aircraft.

Then back:

> It takes others who can translate what's really happening. Especially with social issues. Like Salvadora Katosang who came and helped the women translate what was going on…If not, then we don't know because those who know are not telling the truth. If we don't see the other side of the picture, then we're just being fooled and we can get into something that may be injustice. They were in the group that protested. They called it Save Belau

organization. They were the first sort of radicals. In the 70s, they wanted to do a refinery of sorts in the northern island. They said no. It was a really beautiful bird sanctuary. They were going to destroy it. It was a paper company that wanted to come in but then it was also a military thing. It was later that we knew.

After the War Talk, the 63-year-old woman leans forward to demarcate the most vital coordinates of all. Where education can be about liberation.

I see two baskets: a Palauan cultural basket, and a western basket. This cultural basket makes me a Palauan. Whatever is in this basket, we need to develop more. Without this basket, I don't think we'll be good people living on this island. This island was developed by Palauans, and we were developed by this island in turn. In Belau, one of the things we value most is the interrelationship among relatives, community members, etc. It is not being developed because a concept of individualism is replacing it.

The western basket has tools, not culture. I can use pick and choose whatever tools in the second basket that could enhance my own. Just like a wrench, a knife and fork. I can use these tools to make my work easy. The danger I see right now is that we're putting away our cultural basket and using the tools as a replacement of our culture. It is everybody's fault—parents are not training their children, the school does not teach it, and the leaders of both the traditional and the western government are too busy with the second basket.

Another long time activist, 57, weighs in:

> In my talks, I ask these kids: 'Who is a Palauan?' Man, it's blank. 'Is Palauan brown skin, curly hair, chewing betel nut, wearing slippers?' Very few define Palauan as inside. They describe outside. This is dangerous.

Then, as if identity and development are interchangeable politics, this man continues:

> We need to be smart. We need to make sure that our internal development as a people is consistent with our basic values of mutual help and cooperation, respect for elders and people, taking care of each other, whatever we have we share, our cultural responsibilities. The right to speak out is so important. In a small society like this, there are times when we really need to speak out. You have to be selective in what happens here. We developed here for 3,000 years for a reason. Life was hard but our

culture survived because there are some basic values in life, basic principles that are correct and right for us. May not be right for others.

Then, with the floodgate flung open, came the water:

One thing we should do is get the community to come up with its own vision statement. I'm asking people to form a group and encouraging them to take power of their own resources and think about what they can do with what they have. For example, Kayangel State can sit down and come up with a community company that makes salt. For me, I don't like the tourism industry because we're so busy serving people all the time. I want the community to be able to tell people what to do. I really don't like this eco-tourism thing because we're going to be slaves forever. That's a good way to keep us down. I say to them: 'I'm not from Kayangel, so I should not plan for you. But take hold of your own resources and think. Maybe you can export salt to Yap. Just go and see how much salt they bring in on the ship. And we can make this. You can make it.' 'Ngardmau: you can make water and export it.' If we all do that, if all 16 states get up and do these things, we're going to be independent. But as long as we sit back and wait on the national government—and the national government looks to the U.S.—for how long? One thing I've learned these past years is that we cannot

111

continue to fight and fight and not have some kind of alternative idea in mind. I see this community visioning project as one possible alternative.

...63-year-old Palauan woman.

The older woman joins in:

Like in Anguar State. Now they're talking about bringing in the casinos. I talked to the Governor and asked him why the leadership thinks casinos would be good for Anguar. Most of those people are not educated. Who is going to run the casino? Not the people from there. Also, the people coming as tourists are not coming to Anguar to gamble, they're coming for diving. We should support the women there selling betel nut and leaves. They're making money. Let's develop for ourselves.

Finally:

We need to work with what we have. Get together and develop something. You can put your own money into it. Get a loan. Tourism? I don't want to sit and wait for a busload of people to come in and keep smiling, keep smiling. My face is going to hurt. I'd rather ask them if they want to buy salt.

And the dream takes hold. And the dream has fight in it. Like the women who carried it here.

> We are afraid to be alone doing things. So we need the world to say we are against this and are against that...If these islands, for example, get together and do something so maybe in ten years, twenty years, we have developed something so this is not so empty, so they can come in and take roots here. Right now, we depend on the U.S. for all this. Once we start to be a little bit more independent, change can come from the bottom up.

Love in the Time of Cholera

On the CNMI and Guam

In the 1970s, the Northern Mariana Islands chose to stay in close political union with the U.S. and by many accounts remains the farthest of the entrusted islands from self-government. In fact, the U.S. is currently working to federalize several rights previously garnered by the CNMI. In 1976, the mutually agreed Covenant to Establish the Commonwealth of the Northern Mariana Islands was approved by Congress and the new Commonwealth of the Northern Mariana Islands (CNMI) government came into effect two years later. While U.S. federal law applies generally, federal immigration and labor law including the minimum wage law are largely locally-controlled, at least until now. The CNMI's minimum wage law changed in May 2007. Also in the pipes is pressure by the Interior Department that the CNMI change its immigration law. While CNMI citizens are U.S. citizens, they do not hold all of the rights and privileges provided in the U.S. Constitution, have no delegate to Congress, and cannot vote in U.S. Presidential elections. Unlike their brothers and sisters in the CNMI, Guam never chose to stay in close political union with the U.S. That closeness was chosen for her. In fact, military desire for Guam has meant the strategic blocking of

115

the Chamoru people of Guam's struggle for self-determination. Guam's domestic personality is that of an unincorporated territory of the U.S., administered by the Office of Insular Affairs in the Department of the Interior. The Organic Act of 1950 placed upon the people of Guam serves as Guam's Constitutional document though by no account is it a measure of self-government or expression of Chamoru self-determination. While the people of Guam are U.S. citizens, they do not hold all of the rights and privileges provided in the U.S. Constitution, have no real vote in the U.S. Congress, and cannot vote in U.S. Presidential elections. Guam's international personality is that of a Non-Self-Governing Territory (NSGT). Guam remains on the United Nations' list of NSGTs and continued to report progress, or lack thereof, toward decolonization to the U.N. for half a century. Today, with the current enormous U.S. military expansionism planned for and already begun in Guam, their faith in progressing off the U.N. NSGT list is fading fast.

While the world is still not looking, a civilization born two thousand years before Jesus is up for grabs. Everything must go. Water, wharfs, land, pride, self determination, self respect. Final Resting Places. In Guam, even the dead are dying again. According to the Guam Historic Preservation Office, more than 287 graves have been desecrated at the ancient village of Ngaton for the sake of redesigning Okura Hotel.[48] 161 others for a swimming pool at Nikko Hotel.[49] 500 more were desecrated at the Hyatt.[50] Just this month (July 2007) in the ancient village of Gokna, graves were again gutted to pave the way for a proposed sky-rise and mega-shopping compound.[51] The latest argument from the developers is that they didn't know, however, there was a documented attempt in 1993 to build a hotel in that spot before, a project stayed by protest.[52] Of course the sting is sharper in our land, as we come from a rich tradition of ancestor worship. In another village to the north, in the island of Saipan, another tradition is being eyed for the kill. In a village carbon dated to 1500 B.C. (plus or minus 200 years), the U.S. is using federal environmental regulations to deny fisherfolk access to their traditional fishing grounds. [53] Designating Laulau Bay as a turtle conservation area, the U.S.-guided Coastal Resource Management has outlawed local fishermen from driving to the shoreline to unload their boats from their trucks to the water[54] though to date not a single turtle has been sighted in the area this year, and the egg-laying season for turtles began in April.[55]

The reader should know: to write about the Commonwealth of the Northern Mariana Islands, which includes Saipan, Luta, Tinian, and the rest of the northern islands—alongside Guam—is itself a political act. Definitely one of decolonization. In 1898, at the end of the Spanish-American war, the natural archipelago of the Chamoru people was severed. The U.S. purchased Guam, while the rest of the Marianas Islands (CNMI) went to the Germans. Thirty years of referenda, in which many CNMI Chamorus voted repeatedly to reunite with Guam Chamorus, went nowhere. Wounds from WWII—when Japan (who took the CNMI from Germany) brought Saipan Chamorus to Guam to serve as translators for the slaughter of Guam Chamorus—proved too deep to dislodge. Years later, the anger and the inability to forgive on the part of the latter sealed the deal. Since, the twins have spiraled in different directions. Lately, both are just going down.

At the time of this writing, the CNMI is imploding. Fast.

Though it long controlled two major pieces of domestic policy—immigration and minimum wage—CNMI in 2007 is set to lose control of both. The Chinese-dominated garment

118

industry that spread through Saipan like a brush fire, with close to forty factories at its peak, is on its way out.[56] Exactly a decade ago, there were close to a million tourists a year. Now, the tourism industry catches less than half of that. The dual crashes of a Korean Airlines plane and the Asian economy in the late 90s hit too hard.[57] Hotels have closed whole wings. Pursuant to a new law, the minimum wage, which has sat at \$3.05 for as long as anyone can remember, has been raised to \$3.55 this month, and it will continue to rise every year until it reaches the U.S. federal minimum wage. [58] Recently, the U.S. Congress has federalized immigration, passing a bill whereby nonresident migrant workers who had continuous employment in the CNMI for the last five years can apply for a status similar to that of the people of the FSM—non U.S. citizens who can travel freely in and out of the U.S.[59] Many folks are concerned that this move will dispossess Saipan Chamorus in their own homeland, distancing them from political power in the coming years—a fate no doubt familiar to Guam Chamorus. Also on the landscape is the Carolinian community, made up of folks from the central Caroline Islands who have made Saipan their home as long as anyone can remember and who continue to feel slighted by the island's political framework. Saipan, the urban center and seat of CNMI government, is a shell of her former self.

So that none mistake the gravity, three notes in passing:

> 3,000 one-way tickets [out of Saipan] have been purchased this summer (2007).
> …38-year-old Chamoru man in Saipan.

> Yesterday, when the 'Joe Camacho for Congress' team was out canvassing in Kagman I area, they noticed that every second or third house was abandoned, overgrown. People here in Saipan are leaving.
> …40-year-old African American man living in Saipan.

> When our economy was at its peak in the '80s and '90s, 3 out of 4 people were bound for college. Now, 3 out of 4 people are bound for the military.
> …38-year-old Chamoru man in Saipan.

And the kids are catching on. Falling. In formation.

At Saipan Southern High School (SSHS), widely rumored to have the highest recruitment rate into the U.S. military of any other high school in the entire U.S., kids breathe the red, white, and blue.

Right now, I got 250 [students]. Out of the 750 students in the school this past year, I got 250. From each semester. If you combine the two semesters, then I have almost 500 out of the 750 in the JROTC program.

From this last graduating class, it was almost 40 out of 165 that joined the military, mostly Army. All active. Every year it fluctuates but it's never less than 25 kids. Always somewhere between 25 and 50.
...SSHS Senior Army Instructor.

At last month's Class of 2007 graduation ceremony (June 6, 2007), six of the top ten students had been in the JROTC program. Their keynote? Secretary of the Interior Dick Kempthorne, who, as reported in the Saipan Tribune, talked about his own humble beginnings as a janitor. Somewhere in his twelve minute address, the lie fell out. He said: 'I do hope you do remember this: You are important.'[60] Of course they are. Just, maybe, not to him.

On why he thinks the rate is so high, one JROTC instructor shares:

Right now, basically everybody is taking ROTC because the principal supports ROTC real good. Basically, when the freshmen come in he tries to get all the freshmen into ROTC. Other choices are music and ceramics. First semester, we usually get about 250 kids. Total number is 200 some every semester. When they're seniors, some can't join ROTC because they have to take the required courses to graduate, but some already took ROTC in the first semester.

He goes on:

The reason now that everyone is joining is because the economy. Right now, I got five in basic training and they're still in their junior year (in high school). They call that the split option, wherein they complete basic training in the summer before their senior year of high school. They have to come back and finish their last year in high school. Then when they graduate they go to the advanced individual training, where they get trained in their MOS (what job they're going to do). Like I said, the five went. There are no jobs here. This is the first year we're doing split option. I kind of advertised it. If you have no job in the summer, another way is to join the military.

Speaking about the military entrance exam, he shares:

Sometimes the Army waives the minimum score of 31 to 21. The headquarters come down with the waivers when the Army needs more soldiers. So all those kids who got 21, 28, 25 [can join]. The Department of Defense can lower the standard to 21. Two years ago, a couple of my students couldn't join but then six months later they got a waiver and went.

For as long as anyone can remember, the Army has made a home in the CNMI. But last year, another cock came home to roost.

The year before last, I had eight of them join the Marines after graduating from SSHS. The advantage of the Marines is they have their Marine Corps. Recruiting Station here, which just opened up this past year. Now they just go down there and talk to the recruiters. That's why I told the Army: 'why don't you just have a station over here and you'll get more?'

It's because of the economy. There are no jobs for them.

Do these kids know what they're getting themselves into? These kids have friends and relatives in the service. Six CNMI boys already got killed in Iraq. They know. Two reservists went over there and didn't make it back. They're still joining. Funerals are back to back. Some parents are very protective of their kids and don't allow their kids to join. Some of them, yes, they're scared, but a lot of them because of no jobs and everything, there's no choice but join the military and get a life. It's sad but there are no real choices. How are they going to survive? The kids, they see it. See some of their parents get laid off. Joining the military will let them support their parents, get ID cards for their parents, and they can buy things at the shopette. At the store, mostly people buy beer (30 pack for $21.50), and pampers and baby formulas and all those things. No gas station. Before, they usually had tent sales where they sell cheap stuff outside the store but that stopped. I guess they didn't make money. I think it's three years now, no tent sale.

In a conversation with one Army recruiter, I learned that the chance of getting deployed right now is 90%. But a more troubling number comes from a Chamoru elementary school teacher in Saipan:

All of my male students, and I teach fifth graders, want to join the military.

There it is. That chilling, now familiar, sound of children crying at the funerals of their imaginations.

Meanwhile, Guam Chamorus have both our arms out, desperate to hold our line.

At the time of this writing, the U.S. plans to flood Guam with 55,000 people as part of its global military realignment plans.[61] This figure is said to include the 8,000 U.S. Marines and their 9,000 dependents being ousted by our outraged friends in Okinawa.[62] Joining the now 35,000 U.S. military personnel and their dependents, we are told, is an outside labor force estimated upwards of 20,000 workers on construction contracts.[63] Word is that these workers will come from the Philippines.[64] Six more nuclear submarines will be added to the three already stationed in Guam.[65] Also in the pipes are a new Ballistic Missile Defense station, a monstrous Global Strike Force, a strike and intelligence surveillance reconnaissance hub, and a sixth aircraft carrier for the region.[66]

Though massive, this buildup only complements the impressive Air Force and Navy show of force occupying 1/3 of our thirty mile island already. This influx will have devastating consequences on the Chamorus of Guam, who make up only 37% of the roughly 170,000 people living in Guam and who already suffer the signature maladies of a colonial condition.

The repeated suggestion is that the government of Guam is expected to foot the bill of this re-occupation. Meetings with defense officials have proved empty. Military officers we have met with inform us only of their inability to commit to anything. In effect, they repeat that they have no working plans to spend money on civilian projects. Dollars tied to this transfer have been allocated to development only within the bases.[67] Home Depot has just opened its doors in Guam. It has already worked out a sweetheart deal with Matson, which will no doubt drive locally-owned businesses to the ground, as did K-Mart when it arrived on scene.[68] Ruby Tuesdays is also breaking ground in Guam.

There is talk of plans to condemn more of our land to accommodate its accelerated military needs. In contrast, there is no talk of plans to clean up radioactive contaminations of Guam from toxins leftover from its World War II activities and its intense nuclear bombing campaign of the Marshall Islands only 1200 miles from Guam. Despite the hard work of local advocacy group Pacific Association for Radiation Survivors (PARS), Guam's non-voting Congresswoman Madeleine Bordallo has yet to introduce the bill that would compensate Guam survivors of radioactive fallout from the NTP in the Marshalls by affording Guam inclusion into the Radiation Exposure Compensation Act (RECA), which has been highly successful in Nevada and elsewhere in the continental U.S.[69] Meanwhile, there's been a whirlwind of articles and secret memos and documents detailing more about the truth of one poison or another having been either stored, spilled, used, or buried here.[70] Agent Purple. Agent Orange. Dioxins. Heavy metals. Polychlorinated Biphenyls (PCBs).

The latest news item falling from the sky is talk of a new super road to be developed for easy access from the U.S. Air Force base in the north to the U.S. Navy one in the south.[71] We wonder how many villages will be gutted to build it. We wait with bated breath as other plots of land, only recently returned to their original owners, may again be taken back by the U.S. for expansion of military-related infrastructure.[72]

In all this, Guam's top leaders look more like rocks than persons, their unwillingness to engage in real dialogue dragging folk further to the end of a fraying rope.

As the unholy trinity—Non-voting Congresswoman Madeleine Bordallo, Governor Felix Camacho, and the U.S. Statesider-controlled Guam Chamber of Commerce—works hard to put our hope in the ground, the Military's Mouthpiece, the *Pacific Daily News*, is coming down like The Daily Hammer. All of it so noisy, so distracting, so manic, so carnal. So Rome.

But our brave activists are also hard at work. Just last week (July 20, 2007), three were petitioning at decolonization hearings at the U.N. yet again; another was in Australia linking arms with our friends in opposition to joint U.S.-Australia military exercises; another in the CNMI, stretching hands to kin there, as resistance should be a family affair. All trying, at increasing risk, to say no. Enough. More recently, in a meeting with yet another Non-voting Congresswoman, Donna Christensen (D-VI), a shamed Madeleine Bordallo was challenged by a group of local women leaders who call themselves *Fuetsan Famalao'an*. Frustrated by their rage, Madeleine blurted out the question of how many of the women were against the military buildup. No less than 75% threw their hands up.[73]

The truth of the matter is that what's going down in Guam now is not merely more of the same. It marks a turning point in U.S. military policy. It means to be decisive. Pack the last punch.

One 56-year-old Chamoru woman gets it spot on:

> Right now, this is a really challenging time. I think the U.S. Department of Defense is extremely resourceful. Of course they plan under the worst scenario and they have a pool of experts to come to the island and say: 'Here's the best for you' and

regardless that the U.S. will claim that they do things under the most democratically way possible, you wonder. Because when a general population's educational level is low and they cannot understand the complexity of military industrial information, it's a daunting situation for people who have stayed all their lives on the island. The U.S. ignores this. Have these folks been exposed to the same complexities to understand what's really going on? And the U.S. has planned this at the best possible environmental scenario, when the economy is really at the bottom. They come in with: 'Yes, we're going to build this' and 'yes, we're going to have this.' You know, I have trouble with that. For any developing country going through that, this is excruciatingly painful. You know, these people have gotten used to a certain way of living and people are moving out with their money and then you come in with: 'Oh, guess what? I have a new carrot you can eat.' And people will say 'oh yes' without even thinking twice because financial commitments have been made and expectations have been established. It is very predictable.

She speaks of her experience as a young woman, first peeling back the onion of war:

My experience early on at the University of Guam is that the military industry is tied to the political status.

129

First, they wanted to take all of Tinian, relocate people, and then it was like, how about 2/3, or 1/3? We're not too sure where they wanted to relocate us, but we said no. The first negotiating team came and flashed up their power point and told us how we'd have concrete houses. They really wanted to wipe off the face of the earth the livelihood of the Chamorus. Where's the outdoor kitchen, the chickens that run around outside, the traditional planting of foods and vegetables around the house? At that time, I remember there were a lot of arguments outside the town meetings. They were saying: 'I want to be America' because America is what they saw on the television and the movies. The T.V. came at about the same time. It was hard for the older folks then.

We had a lot of support from people from Guam and professors who helped us research. We here were brought up under the trust territory and we were taught that we had nothing. After so many years, of course, we started to think that we had nothing, that we needed to depend on somebody else to survive. But then again, we never starved. Of course we did our research on all the manganese and the nickel that surrounded this area. We were college students and of course they made us look like were just a bunch of college students, crazy.

Was it Chamorus against Chamorus at that time? Oh absolutely. It was really divided. Tinian was very clannish. We stayed within our clans. Like I know that the Taitanos, the Aguons, the Castros, were like one camp and we were anti-military. We tried to tell our people that the U.S. was interested more in our strategicness and that they should have demonstrated an interest in the welfare of the people. But we realized how minute we were in this whole country. And we demonstrate that by Henry Kissinger's statement: 'Who gives a damn?' We will always be that.

Another Chamoru, an old man at home on his ranch, cuts right through it:

> Everyone's leaving. For economic opportunities. But me? I would not leave for nothing. I don't like the climate. I love using my hands. In America, I get claustrophobic. It's weird. It's such a big place but I get claustrophobic. It's lonely there. Here, you can walk up to practically every house. You go and people offer you something. Food. Here, I'm free. I can go take my nets and go fishing. I can walk or drive. I can throw net and dive. Fish by line or spear. I'm going on 66. If I go out there, maybe I die in a month.

This worrying about only the economy is not Chamoru. The real Chamoru is not worried about anything but food. That is what I'm doing right now. It's not a carefree life being a farmer or a fisherman. I may be poor in money but I'm rich in food. I've given away a lot of cattle. If I was concerned just about money, I shouldn't be doing that. People come by and tell me or encourage me to sell my crops. Like plant more rows of watermelon so I can sell it. I plant not to sell but for my family. If I have enough to provide for them, then that's enough. I consider myself a traditional Chamoru – I work and I share what I don't need.

...65-year-old Chamoru man.

Then, from the woman again, a final thought. Striking in its softness.

Well, I see the final nail on the coffin. That's about it. I am hopeful that we will wake up. That we will wake up and dream. We were entrusted with something and we're not doing a good job and we need to wake up and say: 'What have I done with all of the assets that were entrusted to me?' With today's technology, I don't worry whether they're going to bomb us. They will bomb us. That's a given. If they want to kill earth, they can do it. They have the capability. If nothing else, we should leave remnants

of our existence, give enough clues for those to put
the pieces back.

It'd be hard to say it better. This is love in the time of
cholera.[74]

What We Bury At Night

Lelu ruins. Nan Madol. The House of Taga'. Across our islands, edifices of our brilliance, our ingenuity, our grace, still stand. Like Pacific Machu Picchus. Four thousand years later, they remind us who we once were, who we are, who we can still be. In fact, no better scientific theory to date has explained how our ancients quarried, lifted, transported these stones. The most educated guess they have is that our ancestors had a deep and penetrating metaphysical understanding of the natural world, a relationship with the elements that enabled them to float these giant stones through the air. So it is only fitting that part of our restoration, our politics, be about magic. About imagination.

We'd do well to start with the obvious: Import culture is eating us. Killing us with maladies deadlier than diabetes, lytico-bodig, even cancer. It is the threat on our children's imaginations, so imprisoned by imported ideas, versions of history, definitions of the beautiful, that they cannot—for the life of them—even imagine another arrangement, a set up in which fighting and dying in the U.S. armed forces is not an acceptable alternative.

An 18-year-old Chamoru boy from Saipan, speaking about the sum of money that goes to the next of kin if a loved one dies in active duty service, speaks of death:

> It's okay. To go and die. If I'm killed in battle in the military, then at least, I can take care of my family. My family will be okay.

Like the women of Likiep, of Rongelap, who go out in the middle of the night to bury their grape and stillborn babies, we too are out at night with shovels. Burying our boys, our blues, our dreams, our tears, our terror—that terror that comes when we are quiet, when we realize that we can't, just can't, negotiate with death.

As descendants of some of the greatest story tellers, the gift should have been given to us by virtue of our birth to them. But witnessing what has befallen us, how we have let others trick us into believing that our stories are not worth telling, are not sacred, are not *real*, has clothed our bones with a cold melancholy.

It is up to each of us to find a way to shake that cold off. And come back in.

ACKNOWLEDGEMENTS

This work would not have been possible without the love of my mother Annabelle Cruz, my partner Ron Gogo, my soul sister Lisalinda Natividad, and the rest of my family as well as the folks throughout Micronesia who opened up home and heart to me. Special thanks also to Jaha Cummings, Fanai Castro, Lola Leon-Guerrero, Hope Cristobal, Debbie Quinata, Kelly Marsh, Linda Yeoman, the Heines, Tony deBrum, the Katosangs, Bernei, Lorenza and Cita of Belau, Genevieve Cabrera, Velma Del Rosario, Viola Alepuyo, and David Louis Bell. And to our grandmothers, who carry us still.

NOTES

[1] Martinez, Lacee A.C. July 28, 2007. "Air Guard rakes in recruits." *Pacific Daily News*.

[2] Ibid.

[3] Ibid.

[4] Ibid.

[5] Ibid.

[6] Debbie Quinata, personal communication, July 5, 2007.

[7] Jaha Cummings, personal communication, July 18, 2007.

[8] Tony deBrum, personal communication, May 15, 2007.

[9] Ibid.

[10] Hickel, Walter. 1974. *Who Owns America?* New York: Warner Paperback Library.

[11] Eisenbud, M. (n.d.). In Atomic Energy Commission Advisory Committee on Biology and Medicine Meeting Minutes of January 1956.

[12] Ibid.

[13] Tony deBrum, personal communication, May 15, 2007.

[14] Ibid.

[15] Ibid.

[16] Ibid.

[17] Ibid.

[18] Giff Johnson, personal communication, May 17, 2007.

[19] Ibid.

[20] Bill Graham, personal communication, May 15, 2007.

[21] Ibid.

[22] Ibid.

[23] Ibid.

[24] Ibid.

[25] Tony deBrum, personal communication, May 15, 2007.

[26] Ibid.

[27] James Matayoshi, personal communication, May 15, 2007.

[28] Tony deBrum, personal communication, May 15, 2007.

[29] Ibid.

[30] Ibid.

[31] Ibid.

[32] Ibid.

[33] Ibid.

[34] Ibid.

[35] Ibid.

[36] Michael Kabua, personal communication, May 20, 2007.
[37] Ibid.
[38] Tony deBrum, personal communication, May 15, 2007.
[39] Giff Johnson, personal communication, May 17, 2007.
[40] Ibid.
[41] Ibid.
[42] Tony deBrum, personal communication, May 15, 2007.
[43] Bob Skilling, personal communication, May 23, 2007.
[44] Rumi, Jalaluddin. December 1990. *Like This*. Athens, GA. Maypop Books.
[45] Andita Meyshine, personal communication, June 1, 2007.
[46] LaPlante, D. M. (2007, August 5). "U.S. Territories: A recruiter's paradise. Army goes where fish are biting. Three of the country's poorest territories lead U.S. in volunteering for military." *Salt Lake Tribune.*
[47] Roman Bedor, personal communication, June 6, 2007.
[48] Hope Cristobal, personal communication, August 9, 2007.
[49] Ibid.
[50] Ibid.
[51] Ibid.
[52] Ibid.
[53] Herman Tudela, personal communication, June 19, 2007.
[54] Ibid.
[55] Ibid.
[56] Sam McPhetres, personal communication, July 18, 2007.
[57] Ibid.
[58] Joe Camacho, personal communication, July 21, 2007.
[59] Ibid.
[60] Calindas, Marconi. "Echon, Jacob top SSHS graduating class." *Saipan Tribune*, Thursday, June 7, 2007.
[61] Debbie Quinata, personal communication, July 5, 2007.
[62] Ibid.
[63] Ibid.
[64] Debbie Quinata, personal communication, July 5, 2007.
[65] Fanai Castro, personal communication, July 7, 2007.
[66] Ibid.
[67] Debbie Quinata, personal communication, July 5, 2007.
[68] Ibid.
[69] Lisa Natividad, personal communication, July 6, 2007.
[70] Ibid.
[71] Ibid.

[71] Debbie Quinata, personal communication, July 5, 2007.

[72] Ibid.

[73] Victoria Leon Guerrero, personal communication, August 23, 2007.

[74] This alludes to the stately book by that title: Garcia Marquez, Gabriel. October 2003. *Love in the Time of Cholera*. Random House.

Also by Julian Aguon

Just Left of the Setting Sun (2006)

ISBN: 978-4-90837-32-3

Just Left of the Setting Sun is a collection of non-fiction essays by a young Chamoru scholar-activist from the island of Guam. These essays reflect the present-day reality of the indigenous people of the island of Guam. This book is framed in the context of an island that exists amidst the many conflicts and contradictions of being "freed from colonialism" by another colonial power in 1898 and "liberated from wartime aggression" by a country that put it under a Naval Administration until the 1960s, and who worked to eliminate the culture of the local people through forced assimilation and nominal citizenship. It is written to articulate the reality of the Chamoru people of Guam as an indigenous Pacific Island culture, an American minority group, and an island threatened by the encroachment of globalization into their lives. These essays will cause the reader to think critically on the subjects of globalization, sustainable development, sustainable governance, cultural reclamation, and self-determination on Guam, amongst the indigenous and colonized peoples in the world, question the value of democracy if it is involuntarily imposed on a people. This book is especially relevant for the present state of the world.

The Fire This Time: Essays on Life Under US Occupation (2007)

ISBN: 978-4-902837-11-0

Guam, an island which has endured 500 years of colonization, is now gripped by the forces of globalization threatening to take advantage of its status as a US free port; a campaign by the local Chamber of Commerce (consisting primarily of US Statesiders) to privatize every one of Guam's public resources, i.e. the island's only water provider, only power provider; only local telephone provider; public schools; and its only port, on an island that imports 85-90% of its food and where private monopolies of public goods would truly make the island captive to the "forces of the market".

Written to inform the world of the plight of the Chamoru people on the US Territory of Guam, this compilation of essays provide the reader with a picture of how, even in America's own background, globalization, privatization, the application of non-representative democracy, the militarization of society, and the spread of a culture of conspicuous consumption threaten to both destroy the viability of communities, as well as the sustainable values and cultures that bind them together.

Other Titles by blue ocean press

Parables of Milk and Might: Development Political Satire -

>>The Voices of the Affected<<

By RAN (2007)

ISBN: 978-4-902837-

Following over four decades of development politics, after the official end of colonialism in most countries in Africa, South America and Asia, it is difficult for the industrial countries to forego their economic interests in the developing countries, which are said to be independent. Their continued presence in these countries, controlling or dictating the trend of economic and political developments, is a proof of the protection of their interests.*Parables of Milk and Might* is a satire on the international development sector, in particular, the relationship between the countries of the Global North and South. The book uses a wonderful combination of wordplay, metaphor, and humorous storytelling to get its message across. This book is translated from its original German.

How To Rule the World: Lessons in Conquest by the Modern Prince

by J.F. Cummings (2008)

ISBN: 978-4-902837-00-5

Following in the satirical tradition of Niccolo Machiavelli (*The Prince*) and Jonathon Swift (*Gulliver's Travels*/*A Modest Proposal*), *How to Rule the World* provides a commentary on today's "Modern World" and the "forces" that govern it. This is done in the voice of "civilization's" greatest supporter, an advisor to Prince. *How to Rule the World* is a modern adaptation of Machiavelli's *The Prince*. The author provides the reader, the Prince, with a methodology of non-invasive influence and control that will grant him sovereignty over his or her desired target nation-state and eventually over the world at large. Through adherence to the methodology of conquest explained the book the Prince will be granted access to the psyche of the target nation's population and will be able to redefine its very sense of worth and self-definition.

How to Rule the World, is written in first-person like *The Prince*, and is a conversation with the reader, leading to self-examination his or her own value system, thought processes, and concepts of human nature. It provides a forum through which the reader can determine his or her position in the world and within their own psyche as 'Prince' or 'subject', and how the actions of both impact on the very sustainability of the human species.

Ordering blue ocean press books:

Individual orders:

Books can be purchased and ordered from your local bookstore.

Books can also be purchased online through retailers such as: the Amazon sites (com, co.uk, co.jp, fr, ca, de) Barnes and Nobles (bn.com), Powells.com, Abebooks.com, Alibris.com, etc.

Institutional Buyers, Booksellers, and Libraries:

Books can be ordered from the following distributors and wholesalers:

U.S. and Canada

Ingram Book Group (ipage/Ingram, Ingram Library Services, Ingram International)
Baker & Taylor
NACSCORP (a wholly-owned, for-profit subsidiary of the National Association of College Stores)

U.K. and Rest of the World

Gardners Books
Bertrams
Baker & Taylor
Ingram International